mettle

TO INSPIRE COURAGE SPIRIT CHARACTER

BIBLE READING NOTES

Copyright YFC and CWR 2014

Published 2014 by CWR, Waverley Abbey House, Waverley Lane, Farnham, Surrey GU9 8EP, England. Registered Charity No. 294387. Registered Limited Company No. 1990308.

Mettle Bible-reading notes are produced in association with British Youth for Christ. British Youth for Christ is part of Youth for Christ International, a movement of youth evangelism organisations in over 100 countries of the world. Please visit www.yfci.org for the country nearest you.

Series Editor: Simeon Whiting
Contributors: Chris Kidd, Hannah Kidd, Dani Knox, Simeon Whiting

The notes on 'The Nature and Character of God' were previously published in *Mettle* Sep–Dec 2010. The notes on 'Fun' were previously published in *Mettle* May–Aug 2012 and 'Decisions' in *Mettle* May–Aug 2011.

All rights reserved. No part of this publication may be reproduced, stored in a retrieval system, or transmitted, in any form or by any means, electronic, mechanical, photocopying, recording or otherwise, without the prior permission in writing of CWR.

For a full list of our National Distributors and contact details, visit www.cwr.org.uk/distributors

Unless otherwise indicated, all Scripture references are from the Holy Bible, New Living Translation (NLT), copyright © 1996, 2004, 2007. Used by permission of Tyndale House Publishers, Inc., Wheaton, Illinois 60189. All rights reserved.

Other quotations are marked: NIV: Scripture quotations taken from The Holy Bible, New International Version (Anglicised edition), copyright © 1979, 1984, 2011 by Biblica (formerly International Bible Society). Used by permission of Hodder & Stoughton Publishers, an Hachette UK company. All rights reserved. 'NIV' is a registered trademark of Biblica. UK trademark number 1448790.

The Message: Scripture taken from THE MESSAGE, copyright © 1993, 1994, 1995, 1996, 2000, 2001, 2002. Used by permission of NavPress Publishing Group.

TLB: The Living Bible, copyright © Tyndale House Publishers 1971.

Concept development by YFC and CWR.
Editing, design and production by CWR.
Printed in the UK by The Linney Group.

CONTENTS

- THE NATURE + CHARACTER OF GOD PART 1 — 4
- FUN PART 1 — 17
- DECISIONS PART 1 — 31
- FEAR PART 1 — 45
- THE NATURE + CHARACTER OF GOD PART 2 — 59
- FUN PART 2 — 73
- DECISIONS PART 2 — 87
- FEAR PART 2 — 101
- THE NATURE + CHARACTER OF GOD PART 3 — 115

WELCOME TO mettle
COURAGE SPIRIT CHARACTER …

IN THIS EDITION of *Mettle*, we'll be getting to know God better. Obviously, we aim to do that in every edition, but particularly so this time, as we devote an entire section to the Nature and Character of God. Let's think deeper about exactly who our God is and what He's like.

Moving on, we'll get stuck into three tasty Hot Potatoes. We'll have some Fun; thinking about what fun is, whether Christians really do have fun, and how to know when to get serious. Jesus says He came to give us life in its fullness, so just what does that mean? We'll get some wisdom on Decisions, too. Most of our everyday decisions don't really matter, but what about the ones that really do? How can we handle those decisions wisely, honour God in them and make sure we follow His plan for our lives? And finally, let's have a chat about Fear. We'll look at how fear can affect us, how to handle it and the (perhaps slightly strange) idea of fearing God. Enjoy!

The *Mettle* **TEAM**

MON 1 SEP

READ: EXODUS 3:1–14

KEY VERSE V14

'God replied to Moses, "I Am Who I Am."'

GOD

THE NATURE AND CHARACTER OF GOD

GOD OF POWER

PT1

I ASSUME YOU'RE reading this because you want to know God better. And I expect you're in this position because, like Moses, you've caught a glimpse of God from someone or something and it's intrigued you and made you want to see more. If you've seen God at work in the world or in the life of someone you know, perhaps you can identify with Moses, who wanted to get closer

to the burning bush and find out more about who God was and what He was doing. It's a good thing to try to understand God, because it helps us to follow Him and live His way. So, this series of readings will look at different aspects of who God is and what He does.

But, ironically, as we seek to know and understand God better, we must start with an awareness that God is beyond our understanding! God describes Himself: 'I AM WHO I AM'. The phrase hints that God's nature is so eternal, so profound, so transcendent that it's impossible to describe in human terms. Our minds just can't take in how incredible God is! God will often allow us glimpses of Himself which help us to know Him better, but this side of heaven we'll never see Him or comprehend Him completely as He is. The good news is that although we can't understand God completely, we can get to know Him better, little by little. Each new insight we get into God's character is fascinating and inspiring. As we begin to understand God better, we're changed forever, just as Moses was.

PRAY

Almighty God, I know that You're beyond my understanding, but I want to know You and understand You better. Please let me see glimpses of You and let me become more like You. Amen.

TUES 2 SEP

READ:
GENESIS 1:1–5

KEY VERSE
v1

'In the beginning God created the heavens and the earth.'

LAST YEAR, WE found out that my wife was pregnant. Right from the start it was incredible to watch a new life growing inside her and to reflect that God was making this possible. Our baby started as just a group of cells. At our first scan, the baby was just five millimetres long. But, over the following weeks and months, he grew into a small person! We were both struck by the wonder of a new life being created. Truly, we saw God's creative power at work.

The first thing the Bible tells us about God is that He is a creator. He formed the earth out of nothing, and brought life, order and beauty. It's in God's nature to be creative.

Sometimes God's creations (us) can forget how we were 'fearfully and wonderfully made' (Psalm 139:14, NIV). *You* were made by the Creator of the universe! What's more, just as my baby boy is very like me, we were made in the likeness of God (Gen. 1:26–27) – what an honour!

Right the way through the Bible, we see God's ability to create something out of nothing, to give life to the dead and to provide an answer in a seemingly impossible situation. God's power brings life.

CHALLENGE
We explored the theme of 'Creation' further in the May–August *Mettle*. Get hold of a copy and flick through it to find out more about God the Creator.

READ:
PSALM 8:1-9

KEY VERSE
v1

'O LORD, our Lord, your majestic name fills the earth!'

WED 3 SEP

A WHILE AGO I saw a programme on TV about a guy who made a whole garden out of plasticine. He got a load of different people to help him, and they made all sorts of different flowers and trees. The result looked superb. But it took a team of dozens of people weeks on end to make it and, on closer inspection, everything in the garden was missing a lot of the detail and texture that you'd find in real plants. And, perhaps most importantly, none of it was actually alive!

The programme reminded me of how incredible God is. Everything He makes is detailed down to a microscopic level, and He does it all Himself – He doesn't need a team to help Him put everything together. Most amazingly of all, God creates plants and animals which are alive. All of these things grow, feed and have the potential to reproduce themselves.

When we take a good look at anything God has created, it reminds us that He is awesome. When you begin to appreciate how intricate and beautiful something is, it tells you more about God, who made it. In everything around us, throughout the world, there is a message that God is majestic.

THINK

Find a plant and look at it closely: the veins on the leaves and the structure of the flowers. If you're feeling brave, dig around it and look at the roots. Reflect on how God shows His glory through His creation.

THURS 4 SEP

READ: REVELATION 1:9-18

KEY VERSE
v16

'his face was like the sun in all its brilliance.'

HAVE YOU EVER seen something so beautiful that it leaves you speechless? A few years ago I spent some time in Cambodia. Towards the end of my stay I spent a day on the most stunning beach. I could tell you how white and perfect the sand was, about the warm, clear sea, about sitting under a palm tree and admiring it all, but my words could never do justice to how beautiful this place was.

In Revelation chapter one, we read that God shows the apostle John an incredible vision of Jesus, which he describes in poetic, pictorial language. John sees Jesus not as the man He was when He walked the earth, but as the brilliant, spectacular Son of God who's conquered death and the grave. You get the impression that John is so stunned by what he sees that he's struggling to put his vision into words. (So perhaps we shouldn't think that Jesus literally has a sword coming out of his mouth or flames for eyes – just that He's so incredible to look at that He's beyond description!) In fact, John is so stunned by Jesus' glory that all he can do is fall on his face at Jesus' feet. When we catch a glimpse of Jesus in His glory we're compelled to do the same thing: to fall at His feet and worship Him.

PRAY

Lord Jesus, You are incredible. You are the Son of God and You are more powerful and beautiful than my words could ever express. Jesus, I worship You. Amen.

READ:
ISAIAH 6:1–7

KEY VERSE
v5

'I am doomed, for I am a sinful man ... Yet I have seen the King, the LORD of Heaven's Armies.'

FRI 5 SEP

HAVE YOU EVER been into a shop, paid for something with a banknote, then seen the cashier hold the banknote up to the light? They do that because a genuine banknote has a watermark in it which can only be seen if you hold it up to the light. If a note doesn't have a watermark, it's a forgery.

God is like a pure light. He's completely holy and flawless, and there's no darkness in Him. When we spend time with God, His purity and holiness show up what we're really like, just as light does with a banknote. This can be an uncomfortable experience. When Isaiah encountered God's holiness it made him realise how much sin was in him and the people around him.

When we begin to appreciate how pure and holy God is we can experience similar feelings to Isaiah. We become more aware of our own faults, and we can feel shame and sorrow for these things. We might even find it hard to believe that God would want anything to do with us. But this intensely holy God accepts us, forgives us and wants to work through us, just as He did with Isaiah.

THINK

How aware are you of God's holiness? Ask Him to show you how holy He is. If He begins to highlight flaws in you, ask for His forgiveness and the strength to change.

WEEKEND
6/7 SEP

READ:
JOB 38:4–18

KEY VERSE
v4

'Where were you when I laid the foundations of the earth?'

ANY NARNIA FANS out there? If you know *The Lion, The Witch and The Wardrobe*, you'll remember the scene in which Peter, Susan and Lucy discover who Aslan is. When they find out that Aslan is a lion and not, as they had thought, a man, they get quite nervous. After all, lions aren't known for being particularly friendly. When Lucy asks whether Aslan is 'safe', the reply she gets is simple but profound: he isn't safe, but he's 'good' and he is the king. This is a valuable insight into God's character, too.

Many people don't appreciate just how powerful God is. Have you ever seen a cartoon representation of God? It usually depicts a good guy with a beard, sitting on a cloud and giving good things to good people. But this description sounds more like Santa than God!

As these verses from Job tell us, God isn't safe or tame. He is awesome. He formed the earth itself and He holds creation together. It's easy to ignore that, or forget it, and to imagine God as some kind of grandad in the sky. But that isn't a true picture of God and, when we start thinking like that, it becomes more tempting to think that God's commandments to us don't really matter. We can find ourselves compromising on how we know God wants us to live.

The challenge for us is obvious: Do we take God seriously? He's not safe, but He is good.

→ CHALLENGE

Think about how you picture God. Is He safe or just a cosmic grandad to you? Or do you see Him as awesome and untamed? Does your lifestyle show that? In other words, do you take God seriously?

MON 8 SEP

READ:
PSALM 9:1–11

KEY VERSE
v7
'But the LORD reigns forever, executing judgment from his throne.'

THE WORLD HAS seen some impressive empires. Adolf Hitler bragged that his German Empire would last for 1,000 years. In fact, Germany's borders expanded for less than ten years before Berlin fell to the Allies. The Roman Empire lasted for just over 500 years, and later the Byzantine Empire made it to the magic 1,000 year mark. 1,000 years is a long time for an empire to last, but if you compare that period of time with eternity, it's nothing. God was ruling the universe before any of these empires formed, He was still ruling after they all fell, and He will outlast any other empires that may rise up.

Our God is the eternal King. He is King over everything and He will reign forever. Whatever happens in the world, whichever rulers rise and fall, nothing can defeat God or overthrow Him. When life gets hard for us, or the world looks a mess, it's comforting to know that a perfect, holy, loving God is still in control. We can safely and confidently put all our faith in Him. He holds our future in His mighty hands.

PRAY
Eternal God, Your kingdom will last forever. Thank You that, whatever happens, You're still in control. Amen.

READ: ISAIAH 9:2-7

KEY VERSE v6

'And he will be called: Wonderful Counselor, Mighty God, Everlasting Father, Prince of Peace.'

TUES 9 SEP

THESE VERSES FROM Isaiah are often read at Christmas. But they're equally true for the rest of the year, and they're amazing words too, so it's well worth thinking about what they mean. Right after a chapter which threatens fear and darkness for Israel (see Isaiah 8), Isaiah prophesies the coming of Jesus, bringing this wonderful message of hope and peace. In verse 6, he brings out a whole string of titles for the coming Saviour: 'Wonderful Counselor, Mighty God, Everlasting Father, Prince of Peace.' These titles give an insight into the combination of power and peace we find in Jesus. He's mighty and everlasting, but He brings us peace and comfort too. He's the One who gives us hope when we're surrounded by fear.

There's a lot of fear and hopelessness around today. People are afraid of many things, like failure or crime. Unemployment and debt is leading people to spiral into depression. But it is not hopeless. Jesus is with us, just as He was with Israel. However much darkness is around us, Jesus offers us hope and peace. He's still the Prince of Peace today. Perhaps you know someone who needs to know this for themselves.

CHALLENGE

What is making you afraid in your life right now? Take some time to tell Jesus about it and ask for His peace. Then go ahead and face your fears, safe in the knowledge that Jesus is with you.

WED 10 SEP

READ:
ZEPHANIAH 3:14–17

KEY VERSE
v17

'For the LORD your God is living among you. He is a mighty savior.'

I'VE NEVER BEEN much good at swimming. I can manage a few lengths of a pool now but I'm certainly not a natural swimmer, and at school things were even worse. During one of my first school swimming lessons the teacher took us all to the deep end and told us to jump in and swim a length. I managed the first part of this equation, but then things started to go wrong. I jumped in and sank and kept sinking for what felt like miles. When my feet touched the bottom of the pool, I knew I was in trouble. With a combination of kicking, flapping and blind panic, I managed to resurface. As I grabbed onto the side of the pool, coughing and spluttering, I caught sight of the swimming teacher, just looking at me. My entire life had been flashing before my eyes – and he'd just stood and watched!

God is not like my swimming teacher. He's mighty, but He cares about us too. He's powerful, but He uses His power to save us. When we were deep in sin, He jumped into the world and saved us. When we're in any kind of trouble now, He's right there with us to help us. God is our mighty Saviour.

THINK

Is there anything you need God to save you from? Or is it enough just to know that He is in this situation with you? Pray about this, once you've thought it over.

READ: ISAIAH 40:28–31

KEY VERSE v31

'those who trust in the LORD will find new strength.'

THURS 11 SEP

I ONCE HEARD a story about a man who got a job as a lumberjack (we'll call him Tom). To get paid, Tom had to chop down 100 trees in a week. In his first week, he chopped down 95 trees. His boss said he was sorry, but he couldn't pay him because Tom hadn't reached his quota. However, the boss said he was sure that Tom would manage 100 trees the following week. But the following week Tom only chopped down 93 trees. So again, his boss apologised but said that he still couldn't pay him. In the third week, Tom chopped down only 89 trees. His boss was confused. He wondered whether Tom's equipment was the problem and asked to take a look at his axe. He soon found out what was wrong. The axe was blunt and dented. Tom had been so busy chopping down trees that he hadn't made time to sharpen his axe.

With all the pressures that life puts on us, we can often find ourselves trying to handle everything on our own. That's a recipe for wearing ourselves out. It's silly to live that way when there's so much more strength available to us. If we choose to rely on God, He shares His power with us. He sharpens our axe.

PRAY

Father God, thank You for promising to give strength to anyone who relies on You. Please forgive me for the times when I try to handle life by myself, and help me to rely completely on You. Amen.

FRI 12 SEP

READ:
ACTS 2:1–8

KEY VERSE
v2
'Suddenly, there was a sound from heaven like the roaring of a mighty windstorm, and it filled the house where they were sitting.'

HAVE YOU EVER had to wait for something important? When my wife and I got engaged, it was very exciting, but the waiting that followed drove me mad. I just wanted the engagement to be over and the wedding to happen.

In John 14 Jesus promised the disciples that the Holy Spirit would come to help them. Imagine having to wait for something this amazing. And while the disciples waited they had to endure seeing Jesus betrayed and killed. They would have been frightened and confused. Finally, in Acts 2, we read that the day arrives when the waiting, the fear and the confusion are over and the Holy Spirit comes.

And what an incredible difference the Holy Spirit makes. We see His power in the disciples' transformed lives. We catch just a glimpse of this transformation here, but as the book of Acts continues we see how completely the disciples were changed. The gaggle of frightened and confused men become brave, wise and purposeful. The brilliant news for us is that God's power is available to us through the Holy Spirit, just as it was for the disciples.

CHALLENGE
Ask the Holy Spirit to fill you and transform you. As He works in your life, He will make you more like Jesus. But are you willing to let Him do that?

PT1

READ:
PSALM 16:1-11

KEY VERSE
V11

'You will show me the way of life, granting me the joy of your presence and the pleasures of living with you forever.'

FUN
TRUE JOY

WEEKEND 13/14 SEP

WHEN WAS THE last time you laughed? I don't mean that polite little giggle, but rather the laughter that makes your eyes water, your stomach hurt and leaves you fearing that you might wet yourself. This kind of laughter is great! It makes you feel wonderful and it's fantastic for your health. They say it reduces stress, improves your immune system, lowers blood

CONTINUED ▶

CONTINUED▶

pressure, reduces pain and protects your heart. When I became a Christian my greatest fear was that I would never experience laughter like that again. Becoming a Christian was amazing, but I also knew that the fun things that used to cause me to laugh like that would have to stop if I was going to live like a true Christian. Also, people I knew in church didn't seem to have much fun. It seemed that they'd studied the Bible and found that fun and laughter were forbidden in the Christian faith. How happy I was to find this verse! My fear of life as a dull Christian was completely removed by this truth. Life with God grants real joy and real pleasure. God wants His children to be happy and to live life to the full – just as any good father does. After all, He did create the important health benefits that come with laughter, so why would He want us to keep away from having a healthy sense of fun?

THINK

Do you spend enough time with God to experience a life of joy and the pleasures He is waiting to give you? Or, do you make a poor attempt at having fun – trying to enjoy what the world offers and just giving God the boring bits?

READ: EZRA 6:16-22

MON 15 SEP

KEY VERSE v22

'Then they celebrated the Festival of Unleavened Bread for seven days. There was great joy throughout the land'

PLANNING YOUR BIRTHDAY is fun – sorting guest lists, planning refreshments, writing present lists. From the moment you start thinking about it excitement grows and then, finally, the day arrives. The panic that nobody will come soon leaves as the room fills up with all your friends and relatives. Then, the partying begins. God knows how much we love parties and how much fun we find them, so He made them a vital part of the Jewish and Christian religions. Not only did He ask us to have parties to celebrate important events, but His idea of parties was always going to be bigger than anything we could imagine. In this case the Jews had been held captive in Babylon (modern-day Iraq) for 70 years. When the army from Persia came and defeated the Babylonians, the Jews were allowed to return to their home in Jerusalem. There they found everything ruined, yet through hard work and the eventual support from the King of Assyria, they rebuilt the place in which they once worshipped God – the Temple. What an amazing reason to celebrate – and they did it in real style for seven days!

PRAY

Thank You, God, that You give us opportunities to have great fun and to celebrate wonderful things. Please help us to include You in our celebrations and to give You praise for what You have given us. Amen.

READ:
ACTS 2:43-47

TUES 16 SEP

KEY VERSE
v46

'They worshiped together at the Temple each day, met in homes ... and shared their meals with great joy and generosity'

FROM THE BEGINNING of creation God has made sure that people are brought together, whether through romance, family ties, national identity or even just as groups of friends. God knows the importance that other people have in our lives. Without others around, we can lose our direction and motivation, quickly becoming disheartened. Yet with others we have much more potential to be inspired, having the confidence to take on new challenges. With friends around, we seem to be able to have fun and experience happiness incredibly naturally. Jesus formed a group of friends that He could inspire and encourage as well as relax and have fun with. When He went back to heaven, the disciples stuck together through the hard times and were therefore together on the day of Pentecost when the Holy Spirit came and the amazing times began. On that day, Peter preached to an enormous crowd and about 3,000 new believers joined this newly formed Church. They encouraged each other in their walk with God, spending their free time together also. They must have had so much fun – and great joy as they saw the Church growing at a rapid rate.

PRAY

How do you view meeting with people from church? Is it a fun experience or a chore for you? Pray that God gives you opportunities to make church a fun experience for you and for those you introduce to your church.

READ:
1 SAMUEL 17:1–33

KEY VERSE v33

'There's no way you can fight this Philistine and possibly win! You're only a boy, and he's been a man of war since his youth.'

WED 17 SEP

WHAT MAKES YOU fearful? I once stayed with my youth group at another church for a whole week. One night, after the young people had gone to bed, my friend and I were chatting when suddenly she screamed and ran out. This was a little unusual, so I went out to find her. 'There's a mouse!' she cried. Huge upheaval followed amongst the youth group, but my fearful friend wasn't much help as she now refused to come back into the building. A little furry mouse had managed to paralyse her with fear. Fear can prevent us from doing anything. David, in this passage, knew that he didn't have to fear anything because God was with him. He had good reason to be afraid: he was just a boy and Goliath was the Philistine champion. But David trusted God. He knew that what Goliath was saying angered God and he spoke out against it – yet the rest of the Israelites were scared and didn't like David telling them. When you know that God is with you, are safe to try new things within His guidelines. You don't need to be afraid. New things bring opportunities for discovering new experiences of fun.

→ CHALLENGE

We can miss out on so much when we allow fear to get in the way. What new challenges are you avoiding or what new experiences of fun could be waiting for you, if you simply trusted God to be there for you?

THURS 18 SEP

READ:
1 SAMUEL 17:33–52

KEY VERSE
v40

'He picked up five smooth stones from a stream and put them into his shepherd's bag.'

YESTERDAY WE READ about David's encounter with his brothers, a lot of scared Israelites and a big guy called Goliath. Today we read that the story ends well – for all but Goliath and the Philistines! How did the situation change from fear to celebration? David knew God, he knew himself, and he had confidence in both. This confidence didn't just arrive overnight, but over a period of different experiences: being anointed as God's chosen one; late nights, alone, looking after sheep; chasing wild animals away and practising stone-throwing. David took the opportunity to be himself: to stand up for God and to stand out from the crowd – with his own skills. Though the situation was very different to any he had faced before, he was willing to be different from others and try it. This step was the first of many to becoming one of the greatest kings Israel ever had! Are you willing to stand out from the crowd and try something completely different from everyone else? It could release a whole new area of fun for you!

THINK

Read through Psalm 139. Pray that God will help you to understand yourself more fully and become more confident in who He created you to be. Read it again – God really does know you, He really values you and He wants you to be yourself, whatever that means. Be confident in where you find fun – enjoy being yourself!

READ:
JOEL 2:21-24

KEY VERSE v23

'Rejoice, you people of Jerusalem! Rejoice in the LORD your God! For the rain he sends demonstrates his faithfulness.'

FRI 19 SEP

STOP WHAT YOU are doing, right now, and head outside! Or, if you can't, go to a window. Take a deep breath. How does it feel to have fresh air going in and out of your lungs? Oxygen enables every part of your body to function and is there when you breathe in fresh air because God provides us with it. Find a leafy plant. Use as many senses as you can to study its intricate structure. Look at the markings and the veins. Feel whether it is waxy or fluffy, rough or smooth. Smell it to find out if it has an aroma. Seek out an insect or a worm. Notice how carefully it is made even though it is so tiny and delicate. Watch it as it goes about its intense journey, working so hard to keep its body moving. Without air to breathe we would die. Without leafy plants our environment would not exist. Without insects and worms our eco-system would not continue. God has created an amazing world that enables us to do so much more than just survive. Everything is carefully designed so that we can relax and have fun in it.

CHALLENGE

Sit outside for a while and experience the world God created for you to have fun in. Allow your senses to appreciate the different sounds, sights and smells. Focus your thoughts on how God prepared such a wonderful world for you to enjoy. Then thank Him for it!

WEEKEND
20/21 SEP

READ:
LUKE 15:11–24

KEY VERSE
v24

'"for this son of mine was dead and has now returned to life. He was lost, but now he is found." So the party began.'

BOUNDARIES AND RESTRICTIONS are never easy to live with. From the smallest child having a tantrum to the oldest person having to learn to walk using a frame, we all find it hard to be told how to do things. If we find boundaries so difficult to live with, why then do we have them? Boundaries are there to keep us safe and to protect us from harm. This is logical in the case of a crash barrier down the centre of a motorway. Going onto the wrong side of the motorway would obviously cause you (and others) serious harm. However, we find it very difficult when we see a boundary keeping us from something that we know we'll find a lot of fun. Is the person who put the boundary there just being mean? The younger son in this passage felt sure that life beyond his father's boundaries would be much more fun. So he went off and explored this idea. I am sure that his wild living had its very enjoyable moments, but it soon left him alone and empty. On returning to his father's care and family boundaries, he found acceptance, love and a party. In the same way, God gives us clear boundaries as to how we should live. Does He do this to be mean? No! God does this to keep us from harm. When we draw close to Him and live life His way, He gives us acceptance, love and a life of adventure. What more fun can we ask for than this?

PRAY

Thank You, God, for loving me so much that You want me to be safe, happy and secure. Please let me see Your boundaries as ways to achieve a happy, fun life rather than something You are putting in my way to spoil my fun. Let me have fun in Your safety, and freedom within Your boundaries. Amen.

MON 22 SEP

READ:
PHILIPPIANS 4:11–13

KEY VERSE
v12

'I know how to live on almost nothing or with everything. I have learned the secret of living in every situation'

SITTING ON THE rollercoaster, your heart beats fast. The excitement has been building as you queued, and now you are sitting there, waiting to go. You feel the judder of machinery, and off you go. Air rushes past your face, the g-force pushes back your cheeks, and your stomach flips as you turn upside down. Then, it's all over. What are you thinking now? Are you going over the twists and turns in your mind or are you racing to find an even bigger, scarier ride? Searching for the next high means that you never appreciate the fun you are having at any one moment. Looking back, you might suddenly realise that you haven't had much fun because you haven't taken the time to appreciate each enjoyable experience. Paul says he is happy, not because he has everything, but because with God he can find fun in everything. Even if Paul has nothing – not even enough to eat – God lets him see the excitement in that situation. So, try to take time to be satisfied and appreciate what you do have, savouring every minute of your life on earth.

CHALLENGE

In your life, God gives you many wonderful and varied opportunities to have fun. How are you going to ensure that you make the most of each of these opportunities? What things will help you do this?

READ:
GENESIS 2:20–25

KEY VERSE
v24

'This explains why a man leaves his father and mother and is joined to his wife, and the two are united into one.'

TUES 23 SEP

THE BEGINNING OF a new romantic relationship is great fun. Talking for hours on the phone – even when you've spent all day together – is so exciting! As the relationship develops, you go on amazing dates and just spend time being together. Years down the line, you may actually choose to get married. When you do, what fun awaits! You get to enjoy sex with the person you love. You feel completely safe being naked and intimate with that one special person. In Genesis, we learn that God designed romantic relationships to be fun. Yet we need to be wise when we enter into a romantic relationship. If the physical stuff takes place before marriage, then we step outside of the protective boundaries God gave us. He intended sex to be fun. It's a gift from Him, so He gives us guidelines as to how to handle it: within the safety of marriage. God longs for people not to have sex outside of marriage because He knows that, if we do, unwanted pregnancies occur, sexually-transmitted diseases can be caught and we're more likely to suffer heartbreak and sadness.

THINK

You were made by an awesome God – One who spent time designing and creating you. He longs for you to enjoy sex within the safety of marriage. He doesn't want you emotionally scarred by being this intimate with someone you're not married to.

WED 24 SEP

READ:
JOHN 21:1–14

KEY VERSE
v3

'Simon Peter said, "I'm going fishing."
"We'll come, too," they all said.'

FRIENDS, MATES, YOUR buddies, your pals – whatever you call them – your friends say a lot about you. Friends can dictate the fun you have, your fashion style or even your taste in music. What they like may affect the fun you have on a Friday night. What they say may encourage how you think about life. Friendships that encourage good behaviour, cause laughter and bring out the best in people are the sort of friendships God planned for us. Friends that support each other in a crisis are the people you want to have around you. The disciples knew this. Even after Jesus' death, they still hung out with each other because they needed support. They'd experienced dramatic, fun and miraculous highs whilst hanging out with Jesus. Yet, because of His crucifixion, they had tasted an awful, bitter low. Since then, Jesus had appeared twice to them – apparently alive again! They were confused. What would they do now? They didn't know what the future held, so they decided to just love and support one another by returning to what many of them knew best – fishing!

CHALLENGE
Does your idea of fun with your friends fit with God's idea of fun? As well as having fun with your friends, are you there for them when life hits a bad patch? How can fun with your friends help you get through difficult times?

READ:
PHILIPPIANS 4:4-9

KEY VERSE v8

'Fix your thoughts on what is true, and honorable, and right, and pure, and lovely, and admirable.'

THURS 25 SEP

YOUR BRAIN IS fried from a hard day's work. You come home, grab some food, then you sit down. What do you do next? Are you the sort of person who reads a book? Maybe you put on a computer game or watch a film? Exercising your imagination is a great way to relieve stress. It is so much fun to let your mind wander into the silliness and excitement that you can't always experience in real life. Jesus regularly used His imagination and storytelling skills to help us understand more about the Father and about heaven. How are you using your imagination? When we use our minds, we must be careful about what actually fills our thoughts. Fill your mind with positive things and you'll be encouraged and inspired. Fill it with violence, sexual images or hateful thoughts, and your life will have an increased potential for displaying negative attitudes. Also, when we are having fun and using our imagination, we must guard against losing ourselves in our thought lives. Our God-given imagination is a powerful tool, which we need to use carefully.

PRAY

Dear God, thank You for giving me an amazing imagination that enables me to have fun, to think creatively and to worship You. Please protect my thoughts and imagination from harm by helping me to use my thought life wisely. Amen.

FRI 26 SEP

READ:
PSALM 139:13–16

KEY VERSE
v13

'You made all the delicate, inner parts of my body and knit me together in my mother's womb.'

TAKE OFF YOUR shoes and socks. If you can, wiggle your toes. Watch how they move. Think about how they feel. How hard was it for you to move them? Now, bring your hand to your face and move your fingers gently over your forehead, feeling the smooth skin, the bumps and the creases. Feel the soft warmth of your breath on your hand and stop to consider all of the amazing things that happen in your body without you even thinking about it. You are awesome! God gave you this amazing physical body. He wanted you to have fun learning all about it and the amazing things you can do with it, yet do you use it properly? God gave you a personality and sense of humour but do you use these to please Him? God gave you a heart so that you could love and care for others, but do you just use it to hold resentment against people – even planning revenge? You have a beautiful body designed by God, so do you use it in a way that honours Him? God had fun designing and creating you. Life was meant to be fun, but do you have fun worshipping and living for Him?

THINK

You're a work of art made by the greatest Artist there could ever be. Living to please God is the greatest and most fun thing you could ever do with your life. Being a Christian is not easy, but it's a life of adventure with a whole heap of fun thrown in.

READ:
COLOSSIANS 1:3–14

KEY VERSE V9

'We ask God to give you complete knowledge of his will and to give you spiritual wisdom and understanding.'

WEEKEND 27/28 SEP

PT1
DECISIONS
HOW GOD GUIDES

ALL OF US are faced with choices in life. From what to have for breakfast, to what subjects to take at school, to whether or not we should ask someone out; decisions can have a range of consequences. Over the next two weeks we are going to be looking at how God guided a number of people in the Bible with regard to decision-making and the future.

I love the prayer in today's passage. Imagine someone praying in this way for you. Today's key verse

CONTINUED»

CONTINUED»

asks that God would give 'complete knowledge of his will' and 'spiritual wisdom and understanding', and we have been praying that God would do this for you as you complete this series of Bible-reading notes. But why should you want this? The passage says that this is so that 'the way you live will always honor and please the Lord, and your lives will produce every kind of good fruit. All the while, you will grow as you learn to know God better and better' (v10).

As we make decisions about our life, we should be trying to live out God's will for us. Paul tells us in his letter to the Romans that 'God's will for you ... is good and pleasing and perfect' (Rom. 12:2). If God's will for us is all these things, then it should be our greatest desire to live out His will for our lives.

As you explore the different ways in which God guides His people through the next few Bible readings, we hope that you will discover how He also wants to guide you in your own life. We hope that you will see that God does have a plan for you and that His plan truly is the best plan for your life.

THINK
In what ways has God guided you in the past? In what areas would you like to see Him guide you now?

READ:
1 KINGS 3:3–14

KEY VERSE
v10

'The Lord was pleased that Solomon had asked for wisdom.'

MON 29 SEP

AS WE START to look at how people in the Bible made decisions, let's look at Solomon. In the previous chapter, Solomon was challenged by his father, David, to live God's way. We read in today's passage that the Lord appears before Solomon and asks him what He should give him. At a moment like this, I'd start thinking through my dream list!

Have you ever played the game where you decide how you'd spend £1 million? I start listing off things like a sports car, Sky Sports (so I can watch the mighty Liverpool), a second home (so we can go on holiday for free), and so on. But in the Bible we read that Solomon turns around and asks for wisdom. He doesn't ask for riches or for success. He doesn't ask for his situation to be changed or for suffering to stop. Very simply, Solomon asks for wisdom to lead his kingdom.

Wisdom isn't the same as knowledge. Our knowledge is all the facts we know; the things stored in our brains. Wisdom is different. It's the ability to understand the choices that face us, from the facts we have learned, and to see the best way forward.

CHALLENGE
If God were to appear before you offering you anything you wanted, what would you ask Him for?

TUES 30 SEP

READ:
MATTHEW 1:18-25

KEY VERSE
v24

'When Joseph woke up, he did as the angel of the Lord commanded'

I WISH I were more like Joseph. I wish I could hear God's voice so clearly and obey Him so courageously. Several times at the beginning of Matthew's Gospel, Joseph is visited by an angel and instructed on what to do next. His life begins to go through a radical change when Mary first becomes pregnant with Jesus. Joseph is told to stay with her and marry her, and he obeys. As instructed, he also names the child Jesus. Twice in the next chapter he is instructed to 'Get up!' and relocate Mary and Jesus in order to protect them.

Every single time an angel of the Lord comes to him, Joseph simply and quickly obeys the angel's command. He has such faith and love for God. Just think what a difference it would make to the world if all of us listened to God like Joseph and were as quick to obey Him and act.

I pray that I'll become more like Joseph: sensitive to God's speaking and obedient to His commands. I pray that I'll learn to make decisions based on God's leading. I pray the same for you.

PRAY

Lord, help me to hear Your commands for my life. Help me then to act on Your commands with the same faith as Joseph. Amen.

READ:
RUTH 1:1–18

KEY VERSE v18

'When Naomi saw that Ruth was determined to go with her, she said nothing more.'

WED 1 OCT

SOMETIMES WE MAKE a decision that might not make sense to those around us, and yet we know that it is what God wants. Perhaps you choose to spend time volunteering with your church's children's work when you could be out having fun with your friends. Or you might choose to delay going to university so you can spend a year working for a church or Christian charity, either at home or overseas.

In today's passage we see that Ruth decides to go with Naomi even though it made no sense in worldly terms. While Naomi decides to set out to Judah, where she has heard that there is more food, she encourages her daughters-in-law to return to their own families and tribes in the hope that they would be able to remarry. For Orpah this makes sense and seems like the best option. However, Ruth rejects this opportunity, being determined instead to remain loyal to Naomi. The story goes on to tell how God honoured Ruth's decision to do the right thing. He not only blesses her with a new husband, Boaz, but Ruth also becomes one of the ancestors of Jesus! Even when following God's way is hard, even when it seems surprising to the people around us, it's always the best decision.

CHALLENGE
What might God be asking you to do that seems a little surprising?

THURS 2 OCT

READ:
GENESIS 40:5–23

KEY VERSE
v8

'"Interpreting dreams is God's business," Joseph replied. "Go ahead and tell me your dreams."'

THERE IS A lot we can learn from the story of Joseph. At the start of today's passage we find Joseph in prison. The end of the chapter does not give much hope for Joseph either as it tells us that the cup-bearer, when restored to his former position serving Pharaoh, simply forgot about Joseph. However, if you are familiar with the story you will know that later, after Joseph interprets Pharaoh's dream, he is made ruler of Egypt. Despite the fact that the situation looked bleak, God was there and was able to bring about amazing changes in Joseph's life.

Joseph's story also teaches us that God can use dreams to help guide us. I believe that He can still use dreams today. That does not mean that every dream you have contains a message from God, but occasionally you may feel that a particular dream has some kind of special importance. If this is the case, then I would urge you to speak to your youth leader or another leader in your church about it. In the same way that the cup-bearer and the baker were unsure of the meanings of their dreams, we need to seek the wisdom of others in interpreting what God is trying to say to us.

THINK

Is any situation in your life such a mess that you are struggling to believe God could sort it out? How might God be trying to speak to you about this?

READ: DANIEL 1:3-21

KEY VERSE v8

'But Daniel was determined not to defile himself by eating the food and wine given to them by the king.'

FRI 3 OCT

DANIEL AND HIS friends were chosen to be trained as servants to the king. This was a real opportunity for Daniel, but at every step throughout the process he was challenged as to how he would live – obeying the people in power over him or living God's way.

In today's reading we see that Daniel chose to follow God's commands and not eat the food given to him by the king, knowing that it had been sacrificed to an idol.

Later on, Daniel and his friends have to choose between compromising on their belief that only God is worth worshipping, and facing apparent certain death. They again decide to obey God, even under terrible pressure, and find that He comes through for them and rescues them.

We can sometimes find ourselves under similar pressure. Do we stick to following God and risk getting a hard time from people around us? Or do we 'go with the flow' for an easy life and compromise on what we know is right? Deciding to obey God is not always easy, but God is always there to help us live His way.

THINK

What decisions are you facing where you need to choose between obeying God and obeying people? Ask God to help you in the same way that He helped Daniel.

WEEKEND
4/5 OCT

READ:
JUDGES 6:33–40

KEY VERSE
v37
'prove it to me in this way … then I will know that you are going to help me rescue Israel as you promised.'

DO YOU EVER wish that God would give you a clear sign on what He wants you to do? I can remember hearing about people who asked God to give them a sign, then followed Gideon's example in Judges and put a fleece outside! In reality, I suspect they knew what God wanted them to do, but were just looking for an excuse not to do it!

God will willingly give us clear guidance. This might not be in the ways we expect, but we must be prepared to listen for it. I heard a great story once about two boys who were out walking and talking about God. Neither knew whether or not to believe that God existed and so they came up with a plan. They decided that if the next car to drive past had a number plate with the letters G O D then they would believe in God. But when the next car came along and did indeed have G O D on the number plate, they dismissed it as a coincidence. The fact was that, whatever the outcome of their test, they were not going to change their minds.

Our conscience often lets us know whether or not we have made the right decision. While it is OK to look for reassurance from God, we must not test God and expect Him to jump through hoops for us. Often, the little 'tests' we devise are because of our own lack of faith, and they are actually an attempt to get out of doing something that we know God wants us to do. Rather than creating little tests like Gideon did, it's better to follow the path we believe God has set out for us, looking for reassurance on the way.

PRAY

Thank You, God, that You willingly guide us. Help me to seek Your will and to faithfully follow Your purposes for me. Amen.

MON 6 OCT

READ:
JUDGES 7:1-25

KEY VERSE
v8

'So Gideon collected the provisions and rams' horns of the other warriors and sent them home.'

YESTERDAY WE STARTED looking at the story of Gideon. The continuation of this story really inspires me. We see how Gideon breaks all the conventional rules to follow God's guidance for him. He is preparing to fight the armies of Midian, and Gideon has got himself an army of 32,000 men. That's a respectable army, but the Lord keeps telling him to cut it down. So first he cuts it down by 22,000, by sending back all those who were scared to fight. This leaves him with 10,000 men. From this 10,000 he is finally left with only 300 men after the test down at the stream.

At this point, if I were Gideon, I'd be terrified – I'm fighting a big army, and God keeps coming and cutting my army so that I now have less than one per cent of the men I started with. But Gideon's faith in God is rewarded. God continues to direct the battle, giving Gideon the tactics he needs for victory.

Every so often, God might ask us to do something which looks huge and frightening. But when we trust God in the crazy big stuff, He comes through every time – He will be with us to guide us and help us. But do we trust Him enough to decide to do things His way, even when it looks scary?

CHALLENGE
Is God asking you to do something which looks scary? How will you respond to this? Who can you talk to about it?

READ:
ISAIAH 6:1–13

KEY VERSE
v8

'I said, "Here I am. Send me."'

TUES 7 OCT

I'M SURE YOU know the feeling. Someone asks for a volunteer for a job that sounds like a real chore. However enthusiastic they seem about it, you can tell it's going to be no fun at all. So you avoid making eye contact, do your best to look busy or suddenly become fascinated by something on your phone.

In this passage the job that Isaiah is being tasked with is just the sort of thing I would shy away from. God is asking him to go and share a message that people are not going to want to hear. But, remarkably, Isaiah is willing to go. Contrast this with the story of Jonah, where Jonah ran away from the task God had for him, ending up being swallowed by an enormous fish (see Jonah 1).

God has a job for each of us to do, and this job might not be easy or appealing. We may feel inadequate or underprepared for the task God is setting out for us, but the Bible reminds us numerous times that God is with us. God equips us with the skills and strength to live out the future He has mapped out for us. What we need to do is trust in Him and get on with it.

PRAY

Lord, help me to be more like Isaiah, prepared to go for You and do Your will, whatever that may be. Amen.

WED 8 OCT

READ: ACTS 16:6–10

KEY VERSE v10

'So we decided to leave for Macedonia at once, having concluded that God was calling us to preach the Good News there.'

PAUL AND SILAS were prevented from getting to various places in this passage. Imagine how frustrating it must have been. They were trying to tell others about God so why wasn't He helping them to get there?

Sometimes we may have sensed a calling from God but have struggled to carry it out. Perhaps we have misunderstood, or perhaps God has a new task for us – whatever it is, if we are going down the wrong path then God will try to redirect us.

A friend of mine with a passion for politics worked in this area for several years. In his desire to continue in this 'calling', he applied for numerous political jobs but kept getting rejection letters. He was unaware that God had a new plan for him. When he eventually decided to look for work in a different sector he received two job offers in two days. Now, nearly ten years later, he continues to serve God faithfully in this new line of work.

Just like Paul and Silas, we must not give up when we face obstacles. Rest assured that God is there with you, and seek His guidance as to the way to go.

PRAY

Thank You, Lord, that You do not leave us to blindly go down the wrong path but are there to give us guidance when we look for it. Amen.

READ:
JOHN 21:1–19

KEY VERSE v19

'Then Jesus told him, "Follow me."'

THURS 9 OCT

PETER IS ONE of the legends of the New Testament, someone who more than anyone else at the time seemed to get who Jesus was. It's Peter who recognises that Jesus is the Messiah (Mark 8:29). Yet this doesn't stop Peter from making some crazy decisions. We read in the gospels how, while Jesus was being tried by the Pharisees and other religious leaders, Peter denied even knowing Him. He denied it three times, before then realising what he had done; he had let Jesus down.

The great thing is that this wasn't the end of the story. In John 21 we read that Jesus and the disciples meet again on the beach. After eating, Jesus challenges Peter three times with the question: 'Do you love me?' Each time, Peter answers, 'You know I love you'. Jesus then reinstates Peter and gives him a renewed purpose, even though he had denied Him. Despite the fact that Peter had not consistently remained faithful to Jesus, Jesus still wants him as one of His followers and still had a task for him to do.

Sometimes we will make bad decisions but, even when that happens, Jesus still loves us and wants to help us get back on the right track.

THINK

What bad decisions have you made in the past? If you haven't already, ask for God's forgiveness and ask Him to show you the way to move forward.

FRI 10 OCT

READ: HEBREWS 10:19–25

KEY VERSE
v24

'let us ... motivate one another to acts of love and good works.'

IT'S SO MUCH easier to carry on with something challenging if you have someone with you. An athlete will tell you that training feels easier if you have a training partner. If you feel like giving up, your partner will encourage you to keep going. And you in turn can spur your partner on.

Hebrews 10 makes it clear that obeying God, particularly in hard times, is much easier if we stick together. We can all spur each other on to honour God in our words, actions and decisions. Verse 22 also tells us another way to handle hard times: we can go straight into God's presence, any time we like. God is not distant from us. He's right with us, and we can talk to Him and hear from Him about any decision we're making.

In the second section on Decisions, which we will be looking at in a few weeks' time, we will explore in more detail some of the ways in which God may guide you about your future and the decisions you will have to make. But, in the meantime, let's keep spurring each other on, and let's keep going to God with any decisions we're making.

→ CHALLENGE

Who can you spur on to do 'acts of love and good works'? How will you do this? And when will you start?

READ:
MATTHEW 8:23-27

KEY VERSE V26

'Jesus responded, "Why are you afraid? You have so little faith!"'

PT1
FEAR
DO NOT BE AFRAID

WEEKEND 11/12 OCT

HAVE YOU EVER had a truly terrifying experience? When I was a child, my family always used to holiday in the same hotel. While we there one summer, I discovered a burglar. You might imagine that a small girl, finding herself alone with a criminal, would be very scared. It could have turned into a very horrible situation, but thankfully it did not.

All of us will have been afraid at some point in our lives. Sometimes this is for good reason. At other times

CONTINUED▶

CONTINUED »

we might have silly and unfounded fears, like a tiny spider in the bathroom.

Throughout the Bible we find many stories of people being afraid. Perhaps one of the most famous is the story of the disciples being afraid when their boat was caught in a storm. I don't know about you, but I really sympathise with the disciples here. Being caught in a storm when onboard a boat is not a fun experience! Perhaps what is most frustrating for the disciples is that Jesus seemed totally unconcerned by the events – in fact, He stayed asleep!

Jesus was not flustered when He was woken by the disciples. Rather, He dealt with the problem swiftly and effectively. He did not allow fear to overtake Him, but trusted in God and the strength and power that God had given Him. Over the next couple of weeks we will read more about the fears we sometimes face, God's command not to be afraid, and the difference it can make when we choose to put our trust in Him.

THINK

Are there any storms in your own life that are currently making you feel afraid? Perhaps it's a difficult situation at home or an overload of work at school. Whatever it is, spend some time now asking God to remind you that He is in control and that you do not need to be afraid.

READ:
MATTHEW 6:25-34

KEY VERSE
v31

'So don't worry about these things, saying, "What will we eat? What will we drink? What will we wear?"'

MON 13 OCT

SOME PEOPLE SEEM to be natural worriers, always afraid that something is going to go wrong. In some ways, I think I am one of them. I like to check, double-check and then check again that I have locked the house up when we go anywhere, as I am terrified of being burgled. Thankfully I'm not as bad as someone I recently heard about who is so scared she'll leave the iron on when she goes out that she takes it with her everywhere!

The truth is, daily life is full of things we can be afraid of: everything from being bullied to losing something or someone special. But the Bible is clear that we should not give in to worrying. In today's reading we are reminded that worrying about something does not help to deal with the issue. God isn't like Superman, just there to call upon in the event of some great catastrophe. God is with us all the time. He cares about our ordinary everyday fears, so it makes perfect sense to trust Him to provide for us.

PRAY

Father God, thank You that You are always with me, always watching over me. Help me to 'Seek the Kingdom of God above all else' rather than giving in to everyday fears that distract me from You. Amen.

TUES 14 OCT

READ:
GENESIS 32:3–12

KEY VERSE
v11
'O LORD, please rescue me from the hand of my brother, Esau. I am afraid that he is coming to attack me'

HAVE YOU EVER been afraid of the consequences of your actions? Jacob certainly was. As a young man, he had cheated his older brother out of his rights as the first-born son. Now he was about to come face to face with his brother after several years and was understandably terrified.

When I am scared of the consequences of something I have done, I often try to cover up my actions, or perhaps try to do something to rectify what I have done wrong, even if it's far too late!

Jacob's response in this situation is simply to trust God. Yes, he sends gifts to try and appease his brother's anger, but ultimately he knows that it is only God who can save him. So he calls on God, asking to be rescued even though this is not what he deserves.

We can gain comfort from the fact that throughout the Bible, God continues to bless people who don't deserve it. This is the case for Jacob as well. In the next chapter we read that, 'Esau ran to meet him and embraced him, threw his arms around his neck, and kissed him. And they both wept' (Gen. 33:4).

THINK

When you are fearful about the consequences of your actions, how readily do you turn to God and put your trust in Him? Remember that God is always there for you, even when you don't deserve it.

READ:
PHILIPPIANS 4:4–9

KEY VERSE v6

'Don't worry about anything; instead, pray about everything. Tell God what you need, and thank him for all he has done.'

WED 15 OCT

BEING AFRAID IS a very dangerous state to be in. The effect of fear on our minds and bodies can be devastating. On the one hand, fear can paralyse us or cause us to run away, preventing us from being effective. On the other hand, fear can cloud our judgment, causing us to rush into situations with unnecessary aggression, sometimes leading to long-term damage. Whether our typical reaction in stressful and scary situations is fight or flight, it is often the case that fear takes our focus off God.

Today's key verse from Philippians reminds us that our response to fear and stress should be prayer. When we pray, we allow God to speak into the situations we find ourselves in and guide us on how best to respond. God can give us the strength and courage to stand up and fight, if this is what the situation requires, or the wisdom to tread cautiously and try to calm a difficult situation.

That is not all! In today's verses we have another promise from God. God not only takes away our fear, but He replaces it with peace – an amazing indescribable power that 'guards' our 'hearts and minds'!

CHALLENGE
What is your typical reaction to fear? Next time you feel afraid, make prayer your first reaction and seek God's will in that situation.

THURS 16 OCT

READ:
PSALM 23:1-6

KEY VERSE
v4
'Even when I walk through the darkest valley, I will not be afraid, for you are close beside me.'

I WAS RECENTLY in the doctor's waiting room at the same time as the nurse was holding an immunisation clinic for babies and young children. The waiting room kept resounding with the anguished cries of small children who couldn't understand why their parents were subjecting them to such a horrible experience. What these small children couldn't grasp is that their parents and the medical staff had their best interests at heart and that this brief experience of suffering is worthwhile to prevent them from contracting nasty illnesses in the future.

God does not promise us that being a Christian will mean an easy life with no more fear or suffering. He sometimes allows us to go through dark valleys (v4). However, God does reassure us that He knows what is best for us and that He will always be there, no matter what life throws at us. Like a baby receiving an injection, we may struggle to understand why God lets us go through suffering, but we need to trust in His endless wisdom and His unfailing love for us.

PRAY

Thank You, Father God, that You are always with us, even when we find ourselves in scary situations. Help us to trust in You and Your love for us, although we'd prefer to be rescued from a difficult situation immediately. Amen.

READ:
PSALM 27:1-14

KEY VERSE v14

'Wait patiently for the LORD. Be brave and courageous. Yes, wait patiently for the LORD.'

FRI 17 OCT

AS A SMALL child I hated thunderstorms. Whenever there was a storm at night, I longed for my parents to come and get me but was too scared to either call for them or get out of bed.

We all experience fear from time to time. But we know how destructive fear can be. So, what is the best way to handle it? The best way is to develop a close relationship with the One who can protect us, no matter what happens. In the same way as I used to rely on my parents for protection as a child, we should rely on God for His reassurance and protection now.

It's as we spend time with God and get to know Him better that we become confident in relying on Him. As our relationship grows deeper and stronger, we realise just how trustworthy He is.

Today's passage highlights that sometimes we need to wait for God to come and rescue us. He doesn't necessarily whip us away from a scary situation as soon as it happens, but He is always there with us and doesn't abandon us. And after all, how else would we be able to exercise courage if we are not given the chance to really face our fears?

→ CHALLENGE

What's going on in your life at the moment that scares you? What difference does it make to know that God is with you in this situation? Choose to respond to your fear in a way that shows God is in control.

WEEKEND
18/19 OCT

READ:
DEUTERONOMY 31:1–8

KEY VERSE
v6

'So be strong and courageous! Do not be afraid and do not panic ... For the LORD your God will ... go ahead of you.'

DO YOU CRY at movies? I certainly do. Friends and family members tease me because no matter how well I know the film and know what's going to happen, I can't help but cry as if it was the first time I was watching it. We might find films scary or upsetting even when we know that what is happening is not real. Similarly, we can get scared in real life even though there is no real cause to be afraid.

Throughout the Bible, God repeatedly tells people, 'Do not be afraid'. This phrase features a lot in Deuteronomy in particular. But in this case, it's Moses who uses those words. Moses tells the Israelites, and in particular Joshua, to be 'strong and courageous' and reassures them that God 'will neither fail you nor abandon you' (Deut. 31:6).

We know that Jesus has defeated the devil. The victory is God's. The result of this battle is not in doubt! So we should not be afraid: the devil can have no hold over us. But all too often we behave as if this wasn't true. The devil loves to shake our faith and make us believe that God isn't in control. When we are struck by this kind of fear, the answer is to invite God to fill our hearts and minds. His presence and peace reassure us and allow us to 'be strong and courageous' and not afraid. When we are on God's winning team, we have no need to fear the devil's tricks. Perhaps you need to remind yourself of this, or, like Moses, you have a friend who needs to know this for themselves.

PRAY

Father, forgive me for the times when I do not fully trust in You. When the devil is trying to make me feel afraid, help me to turn to You and find strength and courage. Amen.

MON 20 OCT

READ:
JUDGES 6:11–16

KEY VERSE
v15
'But Lord ... My clan is the weakest in the whole tribe of Manasseh, and I am the least in my entire family!'

WHEN I THINK of characters in the Bible who were afraid, Gideon is one of the first who springs to my mind. It is comforting to think that even timid and scared people like Gideon can be used to do great things for God. When we first meet Gideon, he is hiding from the Midianites in the bottom of a winepress. He is clearly very afraid. So imagine his surprise, not only at being visited by an angel, but at the angel calling him a 'Mighty hero' (Judg. 6:12)!

Throughout the rest of this chapter, we continue to read about Gideon's fears and doubts. He repeatedly asks for signs from God and, when he finally does what God commands him (he destroys an idol), he does it at night so that others won't see him. However, we also read how God responds to Gideon's doubts and reassures him.

We read in Romans that, 'If God is for us, who can ever be against us?' (Rom. 8:31). This is not to say that we'll never come across people who don't like us or who we don't get on with. But it does mean that ultimately, if we are following God's will, then being on God's side guarantees that we'll be victorious in the end.

THINK

Has God called you to do anything that scares you? Why does this thing make you afraid? Spend some time in prayer, asking God to give you the strength and courage to do His work.

READ:
JONAH 4:1-11

KEY VERSE v2

'That is why I ran away to Tarshish! I knew that you are a merciful and compassionate God'

TUES 21 OCT

THE STORY OF Jonah being swallowed by the giant fish is one of the best known Sunday School tales. But why do you think Jonah ran in the opposite direction when God told him to go and preach in Nineveh? I always assumed it was because he was afraid of the Ninevites, who were apparently 'wicked' (Jonah 1:2). But if you read to the end of the book, Jonah reveals an entirely different motivation. Jonah was not afraid of the Ninevites themselves, but of the possibility of God saving and forgiving these people who he considered to be his enemies.

It turns out that Jonah's fear was deep-rooted – perhaps a fear that he wouldn't even admit to himself. His fear was that God wouldn't share his grudges and prejudice; that God was far bigger, far more gracious and far more loving than he was comfortable with. Jonah couldn't stand the idea that God was for all people, not just those who seemed 'good' or 'holy'.

Do we share Jonah's fear? God truly is for all people and He'll forgive and accept anyone who turns to Him. That includes anyone you can't stand!

CHALLENGE
Thank God for being so incredibly merciful and accepting. Ask Him to help you let go of any grudges you're holding and to release you from any fear of your enemies finding forgiveness in Him.

WED 22 OCT

READ:
DANIEL 6:6-22

KEY VERSE
v22

'My God sent his angel to shut the lions' mouths so that they would not hurt me'

I HATE BEING in trouble with somebody, even if I know I haven't done anything wrong. Usually on those occasions, I am too afraid to stand up for myself and just take the punishment for fear of getting into even more trouble if I protest.

In today's passage, people have conspired to get Daniel into trouble. The result of their actions meant that the outlook was extremely bleak for Daniel – in all likelihood, he was going to die. However, despite the fact that it seemed as though there was no hope, God was there and was looking out for Daniel. God's supernatural power did what Daniel could not have hoped to do on his own and stopped the lions from attacking.

When we trust in our own strength, then we are powerless. But our weaknesses should not deter us, nor be used as excuses, after all, God's 'power works best in weakness' (2 Cor. 12:9)! When we rely on God and His provision for us, then nothing is impossible. In God's strength, we can be faithful to anything God calls us to, however difficult it might seem.

THINK

Are there any areas in your own life where you are pushing God out and trying to succeed without His help? Choose to rely on God to equip you with His strength in all areas of your life.

READ:
ISAIAH 41:10-16

THURS 23 OCT

KEY VERSE v13

'For I hold you by your right hand … And I say to you, "Don't be afraid. I am here to help you."'

SOMETIMES WHEN LIFE seems tough, we might feel like giving up on God. Where is He when we need Him? Yesterday we read about Daniel's experiences and the fact that, even when it seemed like it was going to cost him his life, Daniel still knelt before God and prayed. Sometimes life can throw us into situations that we feel we just can't handle. But as we saw from Daniel's story, there is a God who gives us hope, even if He seems to be hiding in the background.

It may be that you have no idea how to juggle all your work and other demands on your time and energy. Know that the Lord is with you.

It may be that you're worried about money and how you and your family are going to get through the next few days, weeks or even months. Know that the Lord is with you.

It may be that you're going through some difficult issues with bullying, abuse* or problems with friendships. Know that the Lord is with you.

PRAY

Think about the difficult situations that you find yourself in. What worries and difficulties are playing on your mind? Ask God to show you that He is with you and to give you wisdom about the best way to deal with these problems.

---

* If you are being abused in any way talk to someone you trust or check out www.childline.org.uk or call their helpline on 0800 1111. God is with you and He can work through people like these!

FRI 24 OCT

READ:
2 TIMOTHY 1:5–12

KEY VERSE
v7

'For God has not given us a spirit of fear and timidity, but of power, love, and self-discipline.'

WE ALL HAVE different personalities. Some of us are extroverts – chatty, bubbly, larger-than-life, and others of us are introverts – quiet, reserved, thoughtful. Some of us love maths and science, others prefer art, music or languages. But then, if we were all the same, the world would be a pretty boring place. God made us all brilliantly unique!

Having said this, we can't use our personalities as excuses for not doing what God wants. For example, I can't claim that God doesn't want me to tell people about Him because He made me a shy introvert! In today's reading, Paul points out that certain traits, such as fear and timidity, are not from God. Timothy might have been created to be quiet and unassuming, but not to be afraid and timid. Rather, God gives us power, love and self-discipline, and we receive this through the Holy Spirit within us. If we look at the fruit of the Spirit (Gal. 5:22–23), we will see more of the kind of characteristics that God wants to help us develop. When we are afraid, we need to open ourselves to God and allow His Spirit of power, love and self-discipline to fill us.

CHALLENGE

Read Galatians 5:22–23. When you look at your life, how well do you see the fruit of the Spirit growing in you? How open are you to the Holy Spirit changing you and making you more like Jesus?

PT2

READ:
ISAIAH 57:14–19

KEY VERSE
V15

'I live in the high and holy place with those whose spirits are contrite and humble.'

GOD

THE NATURE AND CHARACTER OF GOD

GOD OF LOVE

WEEKEND 25/26 OCT

BACK IN SEPTEMBER, we looked at God's power. We thought about His holiness, His creativity and His majesty. We discovered that His power is limitless, His beauty is beyond description and His kingdom will last forever. In the next two weeks we'll find out more about God's love. He's mighty and awesome, but He's also incredibly loving and caring. Isaiah reminds us in

CONTINUED ▶

CONTINUED ▶

this weekend's reading that God isn't aloof. He's with us here, not just in heaven. If we're aware that we need forgiveness, if we don't have too high a view of ourselves, God is with us.

As President of the United States, Barack Obama is one of the most powerful men in the world. The decisions he makes affect the wellbeing not just of his own country but of the whole of the world. Wherever he goes, he's cheered and greeted by crowds and surrounded by White House staff, security and bodyguards. But, however powerful he is, President Obama still loves his daughters. He's their dad and nothing will change that.

We know that God is so much more powerful than any human being, including President Obama. He's surrounded by glory, He can create with just a word, and His actions change the world. But He still loves His children. He's still with us. He cares about us, even if we feel insignificant. God is truly awesome, but He's still right here with us.

THINK
God is with you now. Do you need Him to restore your spirit or revive your courage? Do you need Him to lead you or heal you? Talk to Him about these things.

READ:
PSALM 145:8-10

KEY VERSE v8

'The LORD is merciful and compassionate, slow to get angry and filled with unfailing love.'

MON 27 OCT

ABOUT THE MOST patient man I've ever met was a driving instructor. He taught me to drive over the course of six months, and in all that time I never once saw him lose his temper or even raise his voice. This is quite remarkable if you bear in mind some of the experiences I put him through. I tried a hill start, stalled the car and sent it rolling backwards down the hill. I turned right at a set of traffic lights, without looking at what was coming towards me, and nearly got a truck in the face. And then there are the countless times I stalled, forgot to indicate or botched a reverse parallel park. I put my instructor through all this, and he barely raised an eyebrow. He'd have been perfectly justified to yell at me and call me a menace. (In fact, another instructor did just that to me – but that's another story.)

God has every right to be angry with us and to judge us. But He is patient. We deserve anger, but He offers us mercy, kindness and love. However many times we mess up, however badly we mess up, God will always love us.

How else can we respond to such amazing grace than to show others the very same mercy we have received?

PRAY

Thank God for being so patient. Thank Him for the mercy and kindness He shows you.

TUES 28 OCT

READ:
LUKE 13:31-35

KEY VERSE
v34
'O Jerusalem ... How often I have wanted to gather your children together as a hen protects her chicks beneath her wings'

THE BIBLE TEACHES us very clearly that God is our Father, but verses like these hint that God has some motherly qualities too. Here Jesus describes how much He loves the people in Jerusalem. He knows how much they have suffered and also how much they will suffer in the future. Jesus desperately wants to comfort them, but the people just don't want to know Him and, as we read His words, we can almost hear His heart breaking.

Jesus expresses a love for the people in Jerusalem which is tender, nurturing and protecting: all motherly qualities. Jesus has the same love for us today. When we suffer, He longs to comfort us. When we turn away from Him, His heart breaks. I wonder how this makes you feel. For some of us, it might feel awkward to think that Jesus feels this way about us. For others, it probably makes us feel secure. Our God loves us and wants to comfort and nurture us.

CHALLENGE
How do you respond to God's tender, nurturing and protecting love? Do you find this kind of love comforting? If so, spend some time just enjoying God's presence with you. Or does it make you feel awkward? In that case, be honest with God about how you feel and ask Him to help you understand His love better.

READ:
MATTHEW 7:7-12

KEY VERSE
v11

'how much more will your heavenly Father give good gifts to those who ask him.'

WED 29 OCT

WHEN I WAS a kid, Friday nights were special. On Friday nights my dad always came home from work with a bag of sweets for my brother and me. Since whoever got hold of the sweets first generally ate most of them, it became a battle of wits between my brother and me to get to the sweets before the other guy. Some Fridays, Dad would produce the bag of goodies as soon as he walked through the front door. At other times I'd wait until he was distracted then raid his briefcase. The sweets were always delicious, but what they represented was more important. I knew that Dad bought us sweets, not because we deserved them, but because he loved us.

No human dad is perfect, but God our heavenly Father is. And, if even our imperfect dads give us good things, God overwhelms us with His generosity. Beware though: this doesn't mean that He'll always give us exactly what we want. Dads almost always know what's best for their kids, even if that's not quite what their kids want, and God is no exception to this rule. But whether or not God gives us exactly what we want, when we want it, we can be confident that He loves us intensely and wants to bless us.

THINK

What 'good gift' do you need from God? Go ahead and ask for it! Remember, He's your perfect heavenly Father, and He loves you.

THURS 30 OCT

READ:
LUKE 5:1–11

KEY VERSE
v6

'their nets were so full of fish they began to tear!'

WE WERE LIVING in London. My job was with a company based in Birmingham, my wife was struggling to get a job at all and, since we were planning on having kids soon, our flat was getting too small for us. We prayed about it and believed that it was time to move. So we put the flat up for sale … and nobody wanted to buy it. In the meantime, my wife had found a job in Birmingham, so we had to move – even though we hadn't sold the flat!

We found ourselves living in a friend's spare room, with all our stuff in boxes, while we tried to sell our flat in another town. The doubts started to creep in. Had we made a huge mistake? Where was God in all this? After four months like this, someone finally bought our flat and everything started to fall into place. We found a brilliant house, exactly where we wanted to live. And God also blessed us with a great church, great jobs and some great friends. It took a while, but God provided for us in the end. We found that our God always meets our needs. What's more, He provides in abundance – He loves to bless us with more good things than we could imagine. If we persevere in difficult situations, God does bless us. He loves us and He'll never abandon us.

PRAY

What do you need God's help with? Pray about it now. Then keep going! Even if you've been working at it for ages, God can still bless you!

READ:
HEBREWS 4:12–16

KEY VERSE
v15

'This High Priest of ours understands our weaknesses, for he faced all of the same testings we do, yet he did not sin.'

FRI 31 OCT

HAVE YOU EVER seen the film *Freaky Friday*? It's pretty funny and well worth watching if you've got some time on your hands. It's about a mum and a daughter who magically switch bodies. As you'd expect, some fairly weird stuff starts to happen, as they each start to experience life from the other's point of view. At the start of the film the mum and daughter don't get on at all. However, by the end they're much closer, because each of them has started to see the world from the other's perspective and they therefore understand each other better.

God understands what we're going through, because He's seen the world from our perspective. Through Jesus, He knows what it is to be human. He knows what it is to suffer and be tempted. So, whatever we're going through, we can pray and know that God understands. What's more, if we slip up and sin, we can always come to God and be confident that He'll forgive us if we're truly sorry and genuinely want to live differently in the future.

THINK

What tempts you? What do you struggle with? Remember that God completely understands how you feel. How do you respond to that?

WEEKEND
1/2 NOV

READ:
JOB 22:12–30

KEY VERSE
v21

'Submit to God, and you will have peace; then things will go well for you.'

I'M NO GOOD with money. Every month I know I've been paid a certain amount of money, but I can never work out where it's all gone at the end of the month! Just checking my bank balance online makes me nervous, because I can never predict how much money I'll have left. A while ago I got a phone call from my bank manager asking me to come in and see her. I was terrified. What had I done? Had I accidentally spent thousands of pounds

I didn't have? As far as I was concerned, this couldn't be good news. The day of the meeting came, and my palms were sweating as I waited for the bank manager to see me.

What was I worried about? It turned out that the only reason she wanted to see me was to check that I was happy with the overdraft limit the bank had given me. I wasn't in trouble at all. In fact, the bank was just trying to help me.

Each of us needs to settle something with God. We know we've sinned and let God down and something has to be done about it. But God's solution isn't to punish us or condemn us. He loves us and wants to help us. In Isaiah 1:18, God simply says: 'let's settle this'. In fact, in another translation, He says: 'let's talk this over' (TLB). His solution is to forgive us, purify us and wash us as white as snow. So we don't need to be afraid of spending time with God. He invites us to talk to Him, listen to Him and receive His forgiveness.

CHALLENGE

Have you let God forgive you for your sin? You don't need to be afraid of spending time with Him. He loves you and wants to forgive you.

MON 3 NOV

READ:
2 CORINTHIANS 1:3-5

KEY VERSE
vv3-4

'Praise be to … the God of all comfort, who comforts us in all our troubles' (NIV)

A GOOD FRIEND of mine had his world turned upside down when his dad died suddenly. Another good friend of mine had real problems when the company he worked for couldn't afford to pay him for three months, then made him redundant. And my cousin just didn't know what to do when her husband divorced her and left her with four kids and no money. What do all of these people have in common? I'm confident that all of them would tell you that God carried them through these incredibly hard times.

God never promises us a trouble-free life. As we live in a world of free-will, people do and will make mistakes. Other things like natural disasters or deaths can baffle us and make us question where He is in all of it. But when horrible things happen – which they do – our God is with us to comfort us. He won't always make our problems go away, but it makes such a difference to know that the God who loves us is there to help us, encourage us and strengthen us. No problem, no sin, no disaster is so big that God can't help us to deal with it. He can take our anger, our confusion, our hurt. He's always with us. He's our comfort.

CHALLENGE
If God comforts us, He enables us to pass that comfort on to other people who are suffering. Who do you know who needs God's comfort?

READ:
HOSEA 14:1-9

TUES 4 NOV

KEY VERSE
v4

'Then I will heal you of your faithlessness; my love will know no bounds, for my anger will be gone forever.'

HOW EASY DO you find it to forgive someone who hurts you? Forgiveness is a wonderful thing, but it can be difficult. The book of Hosea is an amazing story. God tells Hosea to marry Gomer, who Hosea knows in advance will be unfaithful to him. Sure enough, Gomer cheats on Hosea again and again, but Hosea takes her back every time.

Hosea's story is an incredible example of forgiveness, but the real point is that Hosea's actions were a demonstration of God's feelings towards Israel. The people of Israel turned away from God over and over again and, as you read God's words in the book of Hosea, you can see how much this hurt Him. But every time Israel turned back to God, He was willing to forgive them and accept them.

Today's reading comes right at the end of the book of Hosea. Even after Israel has turned away from God time and time again, God still wants to love and heal the people. He still can't bring Himself to be angry with them. This promise is for us too. However many times we've let God down, however terrible we think we are, God's love for us is limitless. He longs to forgive us and heal us.

PRAY

Say sorry to God for anything you've done that you know has let Him down. Even if you've turned away from God loads of times before, pray and let God forgive you, heal you and restore your relationship with Him.

WED 5 NOV

READ:
EXODUS 32:1-14

KEY VERSE
v14

'So the LORD changed his mind about the terrible disaster he had threatened to bring on his people.'

HERE'S AN INTERESTING one. God changes His mind! He never changes His nature, but here's an example of Him changing His mind. God has literally just finished giving the Law for Israel to Moses (the Law that includes the Ten Commandments). And, while this is going on, what are the Israelites doing? They're breaking one of the Ten Commandments by making an idol! You can understand God being extremely frustrated with them. The Israelites had done a terrible thing and deserved to be punished for what they'd done.

But Moses convinced God to change His mind. Why did this happen? Because God loves His people. He was right to be angry, but His anger is temporary and His love for us is permanent. Our closest friends are the people who influence us most powerfully. God listened to Moses because Moses knew Him so well.

The amazing thing is that we can be God's friends. As we get to know Him, we sometimes get a glimpse of His plans – just as Moses did. And just occasionally, very rarely, we may be able to persuade God to change His mind. How incredible to have the chance of that kind of relationship with God.

CHALLENGE

Get into the habit of spending time talking to God and listening to Him. As you get to know Him better, He'll reveal more of His plans to you.

READ:
ROMANS 8:31–39

KEY VERSE
v39

'nothing in all creation will ever be able to separate us from the love of God ... in Christ Jesus our Lord.'

THURS 6 NOV

THERE ARE SOME things it's just impossible to escape from. Wherever you go on earth, you're subject to the laws of gravity, for example. You'd also have to go to some lengths to avoid paying taxes. And a slightly uncomfortable thought is how difficult it is to escape from being captured on CCTV. (If you live in London, you're caught on CCTV 300 times on an average day, apparently.) But, even if you manage to escape from all these things, you simply can't get away from God's love.

In today's reading, Paul produces a huge list of things that can't separate us from God's love. Problems can't do it, hunger can't do it, danger can't do it ... in fact, not even death itself can stop God's love from reaching us. For death was defeated by Jesus on the cross!

Why does Paul reinforce his point with such a long list? Perhaps he understands how easily we can start to doubt whether God really cares about us. So Paul makes his point over and over again. Nothing can separate us from God's love.

THINK

Nothing can stop God's love from reaching you. How does that make you feel? What do you want to say to God about that?

READ:
JAMES 1:16–18

KEY VERSE
v17

'He never changes or casts a shifting shadow.'

A WHILE AGO I ran into an old friend I knew at school. I was shocked. It was only a couple of years since I'd seen him last but, as we talked, I realised that everything about him had changed, from the way he dressed to his whole personality. He'd never been cool exactly, but now he had slicked-back hair and a leather jacket. He'd always been an easy-going kind of guy, but now he seemed sarcastic and angry. I couldn't work out what had happened to make him change so much, but he quite simply wasn't the same person who had been my friend in the past.

It feels so unsettling when someone we know changes. It makes you wonder whether you can trust them or whether you ever really knew them at all. Well, rest assured, God isn't like this. James makes it clear to us that God never changes. He is good and generous and He will always be these things. Circumstances, our bad attitudes or behaviour – these do not affect His character. We can trust God to stay the same and always be who He is, today, tomorrow and for ever.

PRAY

Lord God, thank You for always being who You are. Thank You that I can trust You to stay the same and always be good and loving and generous. Amen.

PT2

READ: LUKE 19:1–10

KEY VERSE V6

'Zacchaeus quickly climbed down and took Jesus to his house in great excitement and joy.'

FUN
SHOW JOY

WEEKEND 8/9 NOV

WE'RE BACK TO our second look at Fun and focusing on how knowing Jesus can be fun. There are a whole stack of films out there, each showing different aspects of Jesus' life. Many display Jesus as a tanned guy with blue eyes who doesn't say much and does a lot of gazing into the distance; always looking kind of chilled and doing a lot of wise nodding. To be honest, the Jesus they show in the movies always seems a bit dull to me. The real Jesus

CONTINUED ▶▶

CONTINUED»

is fun! Have you ever had a quietly-spoken teacher – one who constantly stops and gazes out of the window? What if your youth leader were like that? Would anyone bother to stay? If Jesus was like this – all quiet and distant – would people have really listened to Him? No way! He perfectly balanced the serious issues on God's heart with smashing through the religious stuffiness of His day. If you listen to good speakers, they draw you in by including stories about real life; making you want to listen. Jesus did the same. He was a fun guy to be around. He was dynamic enough to make people of all backgrounds want to listen. Think about it! A shrewd tax collector like Zacchaeus probably hated religion, yet in Jesus he saw something attractive and fun. Imagine the scene of Jesus – with a huge smile on His face – asking this little guy to come down out of the tree and stick the kettle on!

THINK

Jesus knew when to take things seriously and when to have fun. How can you strike the balance between being serious and simply chilling out and enjoying life?

READ:
LUKE 15:4–10

KEY VERSE
v10

'In the same way, there is joy in the presence of God's angels when even one sinner repents.'

MON 10 NOV

THE NIGHT BEFORE you're due to fly away on holiday you finish all the packing. The last thing you look for is your passport. You go to where it's always kept but this time it isn't there. You tear the house apart, frantically trying to find it. You rope the whole family into looking. After hours of searching, you finally find it! How happy do you now feel? Losing a passport is stressful. However, if you don't find it, you might miss out on a holiday but you can still get a new passport. In today's reading, the woman lost one of her silver coins. These coins were her dowry (what her family would pay a man to marry her), and without a good dowry a girl couldn't get married. These coins were also her security. Losing this coin would have made a huge impact on her life. When she found it she was so happy that she threw a party for all her family and neighbours. When someone becomes a Christian, angels party in the same joyful way as did the lady who found her coin. The more important the item at stake (passport, dowry, eternal destiny), the bigger the celebration will be.

PRAY

Lord, help me to develop a sense of fun and celebration that understands the true importance of things – and the need to enjoy myself when great things happen. Amen.

TUES 11 NOV

READ:
JOHN 6:1-13

KEY VERSE
v5

'Turning to Philip, he asked, "Where can we buy bread to feed all these people?"'

WHAT SORT OF person are you? A thinker or a doer? Do you find new opportunities fun or terrifying? Peter was definitely a doer. He saw every new opportunity as fun waiting to happen. This occasionally led him into some difficulties but also gave him amazing experiences no one else had yet had. It seems that Philip was a doer, too. Faced with the prospect of thousands of people to feed, Jesus turned to Philip to provide a solution. Jesus knew full well what He was going to do (v6), but He wanted to involve Philip in it. He wanted Philip to be part of an exciting, challenging and fun experience. It might not have been a comfortable situation for Philip, but he and the other disciples were rewarded by seeing an astonishing miracle as they simply served Jesus by handing out bread and fish. Jesus brings fun to everyone He meets. To those who love new experiences, He gives a life of fun. To those who enjoy thinking and talking about God, He encourages them to study more about who He is. God is fun!

CHALLENGE

Whatever your personality, Jesus wants you to have fun as you share life with Him. Are you allowing your prayer life to be fun? If you are a doer make sure you make your time spent talking to God active. If you are a thinker, allow yourself space to listen and be challenged by God.

READ:
MATTHEW 25:14-23

KEY VERSE
v21

'The master was full of praise. "Well done, my good and faithful servant ... Let's celebrate together!"'

WED 12 NOV

THE BIBLE TALKS a lot about celebrations, feasts and parties. Right from the beginning of time, God made feasts and parties an important part of the Jewish and then Christian faith. Whether it is celebrating something that God has done, like the Passover Festival, or celebrating something that humans have achieved, like rebuilding the Temple, God has always made sure that we party. What an amazingly fun-loving God we have! In the Old Testament, the feasts, celebrations and parties were started and encouraged by God. Here in the New Testament Jesus tells us a story, illustrating that God invites us to a huge and lavish feast in eternity. Can you even begin to imagine what a totally mind-blowing party that will be?

Our lives on earth are as short as a blink of an eye in the light of eternity. So why don't we give our whole lives now to serving God on earth as 'good and faithful servants' with the promise that we will be celebrating with Him in heaven as our great reward! Let's also make sure that those we meet know of this amazing invitation, too.

THINK

If God has offered us the opportunity to party with Him forever, surely that's an invitation worth accepting. Are you living in a way which shows God how grateful you are for this opportunity?

THURS 13 NOV

READ:
MARK 10:13–16

KEY VERSE
v16

'Then he took the children in his arms and placed his hands on their heads and blessed them.'

WHENEVER I'M SITTING in a fast food restaurant, there always seem to be children everywhere. My eye finds a small child in a buggy. I make a silly face. They smile. I make another. They smile again. Before long, I'm going for the goldfish impression and the child is now giggling like crazy. Their parents spot that their child is laughing. They look up and see me, mid-raspberry. I then blush and hastily return to my burger. Occasionally, if I pull a face at a kid during church, I get stern looks from others suggesting that I should know better; that church should be a serious place where you can't have a laugh. It's a bit like today's passage. The disciples were being too serious. Jesus is speaking to the crowd when some parents bring their kids to Him to be blessed. The disciples want to protect Jesus from unnecessary hassle from people, but they forget that Jesus is a fun and loving man who draws *all* people to Himself – especially kids! Jesus may not have made faces at these children, but He always made time to love and have fun with them.

PRAY

Thank You, Jesus, that You showed us that we can have fun by knowing when to take things seriously and when to not let the cares of this world prevent us from enjoying ourselves. Help us to welcome, accept and love all people, by having a fun-loving, open personality. Amen.

READ: REVELATION 7:13–17

KEY VERSE
v17

'He will lead them to springs of life-giving water. And God will wipe every tear from their eyes.'

FRI 14 NOV

WHEN I WAS 16 I taught a Sunday school class for five-year-olds. One Sunday, one of the boys said, 'I don't want to go to heaven 'cos it's boring.' After quizzing him for a while, I found out that the reason he felt this way was because people die and go to heaven – therefore heaven is full of dead people who don't do very much. Revelation is considered a difficult book to understand, yet it is one of the important books that help us to glimpse more of what heaven is like. The Lamb referred to in these verses is Jesus. The blood of the Lamb is the blood Jesus shed for us when He was crucified. So people 'washed in the blood of the Lamb' are people who have believed in Jesus and have been cleansed from their sin. These people will enjoy the fun that awaits them in heaven. In heaven, the pain we experience on earth is gone. God will, one day, carefully wipe away every tear from your life, so you'll be free to enjoy eternal life with Him. You won't have to waste time on the cares of this world, because you will be free to be with our wonderful God forever.

CHALLENGE
Some Christian things are really hard to understand, but taking time to understand them can help us to grasp more of the fantastic, fun life we can be living now with God. If you are struggling to understand something about Christianity, talk about it with your youth leader.

WEEKEND
15/16 NOV

READ:
JOHN 10:7–11

KEY VERSE
v10

'My purpose is to give them a rich and satisfying life.'

FROM MY SCIENCE lessons I remember that to be considered alive you must have the following: movement, respiration, sensitivity, growth, reproduction, excretion and nutrition. If you had all of these you would be considered alive, but you wouldn't necessarily have a 'rich and satisfying life'. I always find it quite amusing that this verse comes in the middle of a story about sheep, as I've never thought that a sheep needed a rich and satisfying life. Surely all it needs is some grass and it's happy. However, Jesus is using this story

-
-
-
- to help us understand our relationship with Him and the world around us. We are the sheep and Jesus warns us that there are things in this world that will creep into our lives and try to take us away from the safety of the flock. If we stay with the Good Shepherd (Jesus), we will not just exist but experience 'a rich and satisfying life' that brings us fun and fulfilment in many ways. With Jesus in our lives, our spirits are joined with His. Therefore, our spiritual lives are in the process of being made complete throughout our earthly lives. When we become Christians we become children of God, so our emotional lives are also being transformed, expressed and perfected over time by a perfect Father. On being accepted into the family of God, our physical life too is supported, encouraged and guided. As Christians, what an exciting, fun and challenging life lies before us!

PRAY

God who is everywhere, who knows everything and loves everyone, please help me to fully live out the exciting, fun life You have planned for me. Keep me close to You so that the cares and temptations of this world do not rob me of the enjoyment of a rich and satisfying life with You. Amen.

READ:
2 SAMUEL 6:12–23

MON 17 NOV

KEY VERSE
v14
'And David danced before the LORD with all his might, wearing a priestly garment.'

EXERCISE IS VITAL in keeping us healthy. It increases oxygen consumption, lowers blood pressure, improves heart and lung function, reduces your chances of getting cancer, improves mental wellbeing and enhances your work and recreation time. It is a great way to release tension after a hard day or indeed to celebrate some great news like David did. While you are enjoying your exercise, don't forget to focus on the One who makes it possible for you to do so. David danced before the Lord. He could have danced just for himself, but he chose to perform his dance to the Lord who had given him so much to enjoy. David danced with all his might. He didn't just do a little shuffle. At the end, he would have been one out-of-breath, sweaty, happy king. David had people laugh and ridicule him for what he did, but it didn't matter because he had a great time with his God.

God gives us so many opportunities to experience life in all its richness, so take David's example and use physical activity to have fun with God every day.

CHALLENGE
What could you go and do today that would give you immense fun, would allow you to worship God as you did it, and would get your heart racing?

READ: ACTS 4:23-31

KEY VERSE v24

'When they heard the report, all the believers lifted their voices together in prayer to God'

TUES 18 NOV

PRAYER MEETINGS ARE not generally thought of as fun times. They could possibly be considered in some churches as some of the most boring meetings that you can attend. So why do we do them? Well, when we pray, we talk to the Father. He has the power over everything and can change the world with a single word. We're also talking to Jesus, and it's through His death and resurrection that we can be free from the punishment our sin really deserves. He knows what it feels like to be human and understands our weaknesses. Finally, we talk to the Holy Spirit. He is the One that lives within us and helps us with the right words at the right time. When you stop to think about it, the effect of prayer on your life or a situation is huge, and it's this that makes it such fun. You start to see things happen as you tap into this awesome power. The religious leaders told Peter and John that if they spoke about Jesus they would be punished. But after praying they were given the ability to speak about Jesus without fear. How exciting!

THINK

Do prayer meetings have to be boring? You need to be respectful, but if every time you talked to your mum, dad, granddad, uncle or aunt you presumed it was going to be boring, don't you think that they might be offended? Do you think God wants you to enjoy talking to Him?

WED 19 NOV

READ:
1 JOHN 3:11–18

KEY VERSE
v14

'If we love ... it proves that we have passed from death to life. But a person who has no love is still dead.'

AT A WEDDING, you might hear a reading from 1 Corinthians 13:4–7. This describes God's perfect love and the sort of love we should aim to show. We cannot gain it by ourselves. As humans, we are selfish by nature and, without God's help, our love will be self-seeking. This can prevent us from entering into the life God has planned for us, with its excitement, fun, challenges, high points and faith-testing low points. However, we have the power of God changing our lives, and the perfect Mentor in the Holy Spirit, who will show us how to love. His support enables us to love people as God loves them. This love brings happiness, peace and freedom for us and for others. When people hurt our feelings, we naturally feel pain and resentment towards them. Yet, in becoming more like Jesus and developing a forgiving heart, God asks us to let these feelings go. This is the way of true love. As we begin to live like Jesus, walking in the freedom that true love and forgiveness bring, we will be able to start living a rich and satisfying life.

PRAY

Father God, thank You that You love me in such a perfect way. Please let me be aware of Your love for me every day. Show me the love You have for those in my life, teaching and helping me to offer it freely to them in worship of You. Amen.

READ:
PHILIPPIANS 3:12-21

KEY VERSE v14

'I press on to reach the end of the race and receive the heavenly prize for which God ... is calling us.'

THURS 20 NOV

THE LONDON MARATHON is an incredibly inspiring sight: thousands of people covering 26 miles, raising millions of pounds for good causes in the process. The sense of achievement for those who complete the course is indescribable. But every year, you'll find a few 'athletes' who turn up without doing any training. Barely any of them will finish and all of them will go home feeling sore and fed up. The things we work hard for bring us so much more fun and joy than the things that are just given to us. God accepts us into His family as we are, but He doesn't leave us that way. He asks us to work hard: shining as lights in the darkness; working for the family of believers; working to love others; learning to go deeper with Him; and learning to resist temptation. Achieving these things may be hard work, yet the achievement brings such joy and loads of fun. Developing godliness is hard work – but that doesn't mean that it's no fun at all.

THINK

Does any part of following Jesus feel like hard work at the moment? Who can help you to keep going? Pray about this too, and ask God to give you the strength to carry on.

FRI 21 NOV

READ:
1 TIMOTHY 4:11–16

KEY VERSE
v12
'Be an example to all believers in what you say, in the way you live, in your love, your faith, and your purity.'

IF YOU SMILE at someone, they'll usually smile back. If you smile at two people, and they, in turn, smile at two others, then you have caused four people to be happy. By the time you've started ten sets of smiles, you've got a whole load of people feeling that little bit happier! You can easily be the cause of much joy coming into the world – but if you are negative towards people, that negative attitude could have the reverse effect. Many people see the Christian faith as a very negative thing where there is very little fun to be had. We know this isn't the case, because we know about the fun that knowing our God brings. For many, the only way they will get to experience any of the Christian faith is through knowing you. So do you express, through what you do, how much fun friendship with God actually is? It is very important to maintain good friendships with lots of different people but be careful that you don't accidentally do the wrong things in your efforts to show them that the Christian faith is fun. In this letter, Paul is reminding Timothy to be a good example in all that he does.

CHALLENGE
Encourage all of those around you by being a positive, fun-loving Christian. Be an example in everything you do. Ask God for His help and wisdom in doing this.

READ:
JEREMIAH 29:8-14

KEY VERSE V11

'For I know the plans I have for you ... They are plans for good and not for disaster, to give you a future and a hope.'

PT2
DECISIONS
GODLY DECISIONS

WEEKEND 22/23 NOV

A FEW WEEKS ago we looked at the examples of different people from the Bible who were guided by God. Perhaps you thought: 'That's all very well for them, but what about me?' We are faced with a huge range of decisions to be made: sometimes we have no idea where to begin when making choices that affect our future. The good news is that God wants to guide you in your life, just as much as He guided people in the Bible.

CONTINUED»

CONTINUED ▶▶

Perhaps you are a natural worrier, stressing over whether or not you have made the right decision. Or maybe you find that people around you always seem to be convinced that problems are coming and are giving you dire warnings. This is what was happening to the Jewish people who had been exiled to Babylon by King Nebuchadnezzar. They were trying to follow the Lord's commands but were being discouraged by people telling them that the situation was not going to improve. God spoke into this situation and told His people that He had good plans for them – not the disaster being foretold by the so-called fortune-tellers.

It can often be hard to remain focused when all around you seems to be going wrong. It is at these times that we need to look to God for encouragement and reassurance that we are doing the right thing. If you are doing God's will, then rest assured – He will honour that. The Jewish people we read about today would have to wait 70 years for the good things God had promised, but God's promises are always worth waiting for.

PRAY

Lord, thank You that You love me and Your plans for me are good. Help me to have patience and not to be swayed by others who try to discourage me from following Your path. Amen.

READ: JEREMIAH 31:16-25

KEY VERSE v17

'"There is hope for your future," says the LORD.'

MON 24 NOV

OVER THE WEEKEND we looked at how God has good plans for us. However, sometimes in the middle of a situation, we just start to panic. The other day I lost my USB memory stick. I turned my office upside down, searched the whole of my house and started taking the car apart. After a long hunt I eventually found it in my dressing gown pocket – a logical place to put it after some late-night work! I was so relieved to find the memory stick but it reminded me of how we can sometimes go into a blind panic and miss the big picture.

The big picture, we read in Jeremiah, is that there is hope. So much of the world's news today can lead us to panic – terrorism, climate change, violence, economic crisis – and yet Jeremiah is clear that there is hope for our future. Perhaps things are tough for you personally and you are starting to wonder whether God truly does have good plans for you. The good news is that even though it sometimes seems to take a long time, God always keeps His promises. Even though we may waver in our belief, God is always working out His purposes.

THINK

Take a step back and look at your life. What brings hope for the future, for you, your friends and your family?

TUES 25 NOV

READ:
PROVERBS 3:5-10

KEY VERSE
v6
'Seek his will in all you do, and he will show you which path to take.'

WHEN YOU'RE MAKING big and difficult decisions, Christians often seem to use verses like today's to encourage you. If I'm honest, as a teenager this verse didn't really encourage me. It all seemed a bit too 'pie in the sky'; nice words, nice idea, but not really practical. But I've begun to see, with time and experience, that it's true and it works.

I'm the type who often spends a lot of time thinking about the future, dreaming dreams of where I'll be and what I'll be doing in ten years' time. This verse does not say that dreaming dreams, making plans, or thinking about the future is wrong, but that we must not take God out of these plans.

We're told to 'seek his will' in all we do, which means trying to discover God in every part of our lives, not just in church on a Sunday or our small group in the middle of the week. We need to be thinking about how God wants us to act in the class or lecture room, in our work place, on the sports field, in the drama studio, in the music practice room, and so on. As we allow Him to influence our thinking and actions in these smaller areas, He will guide us, in both the small and the big decisions.

CHALLENGE
Where do you need to seek God's will? How can you do that actively, rather than waiting for something to happen?

READING: PROVERBS 2:1-11

KEY VERSE v6

'For the LORD grants wisdom! From his mouth come knowledge and understanding.'

WED 26 NOV

THIS CHAPTER IS one of those passages from the Bible which hits you right between the eyes and makes you realise: 'That's for me!' I'm really struck by the concept of seeking after wisdom, of searching for it as though it were a lost coin. That's a real challenge for me!

If you're anything like me, when you lose something (which I do quite regularly) you will tear the house apart looking for it, especially if it's something expensive or essential (a USB memory stick, for example!). If you don't find it, you start the search again, ripping the house apart for a second time and not giving up until you've found what you were looking for. We need wisdom for making good decisions; it is essential, so it's worth this sort of seeking.

Verse four gets us to imagine a similar focus and effort when seeking wisdom. We should search for wisdom in a way that consumes all our thoughts, right up until we find it – and then we should hang on to it and guard it. Verse six makes it clear: the Lord gives wisdom. So if you want to find wisdom, if you want to make good choices and wise decisions, then ask God for the wisdom He offers.

CHALLENGE

How committed are you to searching for wisdom? In what decisions do you need God's wisdom?

THURS 27 NOV

READ:
PSALM 119:97–106

KEY VERSE
v105

'Your word is a lamp to guide my feet and a light for my path.'

IF YOU'VE EVER had to complete a task blindfolded then you will know how tasks which are normally simple become incredibly difficult when you cannot see. A friend of mine has an amazing obstacle course built into the trees in the grounds of his house. During the day it is really simple and you can clamber around on it without giving it too much thought. At night, however, the course is totally different. You are suddenly much more aware of how high up you are and the consequences if you fell. Similarly, the branches and brambles that cross your path cause you no bother during the day, but suddenly seem more threatening at night.

Life can be like this without God's guidance. The future can seem pretty scary if we are approaching it on our own. After all, we're essentially 'in the dark' as to what's going to happen. However, God knows our future and He has assured us that He is always with us and will help to guide us. He will never lead us into anything we cannot handle with His strength. We can trust Him. God's Word, the Bible, is where we should turn when considering big decisions and the paths He would have us take in the future.

THINK

Do you always turn to the Bible when you are looking for wisdom regarding a decision you need to make?

READ: JEREMIAH 33:1-16

KEY VERSE v3

'Ask me and I will tell you remarkable secrets you do not know about things to come.'

FRI 28 NOV

I DON'T HAVE much patience – I get frustrated waiting for someone to reply to me on Facebook chat, let alone to a text message or email. I often transfer my impatience and desire for instant answers to my faith. When I spend time with God in prayer, I'd really appreciate it if He'd answer my questions and prayer requests there and then. He knows the answers already; He just needs to communicate them to me, right? And then I read Jeremiah 33:3 and think: 'Well, I'm asking You, God. Now it's Your turn to get back to me.' However, I'm not sure that's quite the messaging system God has in mind.

In my experience I know that God *will* answer me – just not always straightaway. He does love me, He is faithful and He does have plans for me; however, He doesn't always respond instantly. He knows the timing that is best for me and will do what is best for me.

If you call out to God, believe that He will answer. It may be in a time frame that tests your patience but He will answer you and 'tell you remarkable secrets you do not know'.

PRAY

Lord, thank You that I can trust in You. I may not understand everything You do, but I believe that You are true to Your word and You will answer when I call. Amen.

WEEKEND
29/30 NOV

READ:
2 PETER 3:3–10

KEY VERSE
v9

'The Lord isn't really being slow about his promise, as some people think.'

AS I MENTIONED on Friday, I'm not very patient. I want things to happen right away and I don't like to wait for them. However, God, in His infinite wisdom, knows that giving me exactly what I want and giving it to me right away aren't always good for me.

I think that if God just gave us whatever we wanted and gave it to us exactly when we wanted it, we would begin to treat Him like the genie from *Aladdin*. We would just rub the lamp, make our wish, and then send Him back into the lamp again until we wanted something else. There would be no need for a relationship; we would just be telling God what we wanted. But, because God works in His own time, we find that there are occasions when we need to rely on God, trust Him and learn from Him.

In the times when I've really wanted God to scoop me up and wave a magic wand to sort out the mess I've created around me, He usually doesn't do it straightaway. He leaves me there, so that I can learn what He's trying to tell me: whether that is to depend on Him more rather than always doing my own thing; to get out of His way and stop limiting Him; or to share Him with others. His timing has made all the difference in my life. I've actually got closer to God through not getting what I wanted! I'm glad that these verses are true. I'm glad that God is patient and like a parent. I'm glad He knows what is best for me – even when I can't see it myself.

THINK

Are you waiting for something from God? What steps can you take to become more patient? What could God be trying to teach you by making you wait?

MON 1 DEC

READ: PROVERBS 15:21–28

KEY VERSE
v22
'Plans go wrong for lack of advice; many advisers bring success.'

WHEN THINKING ABOUT our future, speaking to others and seeking their advice is essential. Other people can show us things from a different perspective, and God will often speak to us through the words of others.

One friend was keen to follow in the family tradition of working in the hospitality industry. She was about to begin a catering course at college, when friends and youth leaders pointed out to her that with her skills and interest in sound engineering this might be a better career choice for her. When she went to enrol at college, she enquired about changing her course. They allowed her to do this – and she has not looked back since.

When thinking about your future, other people around you may be able to point out skills or giftings that you may have overlooked. It may also be that the people you ask for advice are able to give you opportunities, such as work experience or practical support. When you allow people to become involved in your life by asking them for advice, you give God additional opportunities to speak to you and guide you.

PRAY

Father God, I commit my future into Your hands. Please surround me with wise people who can help me see where You want me to go and what You want me to do. Then give me the courage to obey You. Amen.

READ:
HEBREWS 13:1-9

KEY VERSE v7

'Remember your leaders who taught you the word of God ... follow the example of their faith.'

TUES 2 DEC

HAVE YOU EVER been in a queue to take part in some sort of challenge? Maybe it was some kind of assault course or a tricky fairground game. Whilst waiting for your turn, you probably found yourself watching the people in front as they made their attempts. If you did this, you quickly discovered some approaches that brought success and others which went drastically wrong.

It's the same in life. When I was considering what kind of job I might want to do when I left school I arranged to meet with people who did the kinds of jobs I was interested in. This helped me to find out a bit more about what the work would involve, as well as enabling me to work out whether or not I had the right qualities and gifts for the job.

Observing other people is a great way of finding out more about the options available to you. It's also helpful in living a godly lifestyle. How do different people manage their money, treat their friends, and do their jobs? What are the consequences of the ways they behave? Who sets you a good example of how to live? And who could you spend more time with as you try out some career options?

➔ CHALLENGE

Who do you admire because of their godly lifestyle? Ask them for advice on how to make wise decisions. Who does a job in which you might be interested? Try to spend some time with them to find out what the job involves.

WED 3 DEC

READ:
COLOSSIANS 3:12–17

KEY VERSE
v17

'And whatever you do or say, do it as a representative of the Lord Jesus, giving thanks through him to God the Father.'

HAVE YOU EVER been told that you have to be on your best behaviour because you are representing your family or your school? I can remember my head teacher giving a lecture in assembly about the behaviour of pupils on a public bus on the way to school. None of her business, you might think, given that it was out of school hours and not on school grounds. However, the pupils concerned had been in school uniform and were therefore representing the school. It was very much the head teacher's business.

As Christians, we are representatives of Jesus. How we talk, the way we treat others and all aspects of our life will be analysed by those around us, even without them realising it. We therefore need to think carefully about the choices we make to ensure that they are godly ones. I was once told that for some people my life might be the only Bible they ever read. Many non-Christians may never go to church or open a Bible. However, they may be watching you. Are you giving a fair representation of Jesus through your life as one of His followers?

THINK

Think about your non-Christian friends and the way in which you represent Jesus to them. Is there anything you need to change? Pray about this and ask God for help to represent Him effectively.

READ:
DEUTERONOMY 18:9-14

KEY VERSE v14

'The nations ... consult sorcerers and fortune-tellers, but the LORD your God forbids you to do such things.'

THURS 4 DEC

I ONCE KNEW someone who owned a special die which he rolled whenever he needed to make a decision. The die offered various courses of action. I recall that it frequently landed on 'Have an affair'! Obviously, this die was just a joke, but having an affair would not have been a very godly choice to make! Sometimes I think it'd be helpful to have a crystal ball and see what was going to happen in the future. However, the Bible makes it very clear that fortune-tellers and the like are dangerous, and even 'detestable' to God. I have known people who have consulted Ouija boards for advice and they could tell you about some dark and disturbing experiences they've had because of this.

Some of your friends probably read their horoscopes. But the Bible warns specifically about astrology, saying that astrologers do not have the power to save us (Isa. 47:13–14). We need to be careful not to get involved in the occult, even apparently minor stuff like horoscopes. It can seem like a short-cut to advice on our future, but at best it's empty, and a distraction from relying on God for our future. At worst, it's highly dangerous and can lead us down a very dark path.

PRAY

Lord, help me to rely on You to guide my future and help me not to turn to horoscopes or other forms of fortune-telling. Amen.

FRI 5 DEC

READ: ROMANS 12:1-16

KEY VERSE
v1

'give your bodies to God ... Let them be a living and holy sacrifice'

I LOVE *THE MESSAGE'S* paraphrase of today's reading, which includes the words, 'Take your everyday, ordinary life – your sleeping, eating, going-to-work, and walking-around life – and place it before God as an offering' (Rom. 12:1, *The Message*).

God makes such a simple request of us. He doesn't ask us to earn our salvation through great acts. (We received God's free gift of salvation when we chose to follow Jesus.) All God asks is that we make Him part of everything we do. At times we overcomplicate this by trying to work out exactly what role God may have chosen for us. Today's reading makes it clear that we need simply to lay our ordinary, day-to-day lives before God. This gives Him the control. It allows our relationship with Jesus to impact our decision making. Giving our lives to God means making the choice to go God's way in every part of our existence – school, work, family, friends, sport, leisure activities, church – everything. If we're willing to do this, making decisions becomes easier – and the decisions we make become wiser.

CHALLENGE

How are you giving 'your everyday, ordinary life – your sleeping, eating, going-to-work, and walking-around life' to God as an offering? Do you still need to hand over any area of your life to God?

READ:
PSALM 111:1–10

KEY VERSE V10

'Fear of the LORD is the foundation of true wisdom. All who obey his commandments will grow in wisdom.'

FEAR
PT2
FEARING GOD

WEEKEND 6/7 DEC

WHEN I WAS younger, I used to hate getting into trouble. I loved playing cricket in the back garden, but my dad would go nuts if I knocked a ball over the fence. It didn't take me long to work out that I could avoid getting into trouble for lost balls if I just didn't tell my dad what had happened! I loved my dad (and still do!) but I certainly didn't want to get into his bad books if I could help it.

CONTINUED▶

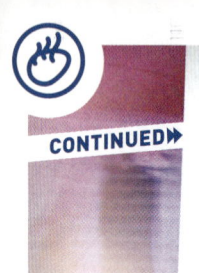

CONTINUED▶

Many children fear their parents in some way but this can be for different reasons. For some it is because their parents are distant and perhaps even abusive. Thankfully, this was not the case for me. I was so scared of my parents finding out about what I'd done, because I didn't want to have let them down. I loved and respected my parents, so I wanted to please them and make them proud of me.

I used to find the concept of fearing God a little bit hard. Surely if God is the loving Father we read about in the Bible, we should not be afraid of Him. But 'fearing' God isn't the same as being afraid of Him, as if He was harsh or abusive. It is about respecting Him and obeying Him, because He cares deeply for us and wants the best for us. In the same way as my love and respect for my parents made me want to please them, we should make it our aim to please God.

THINK
Do you 'fear' God in this way? If so, how far do your words and actions show that?

READ: PROVERBS 19:20–27

KEY VERSE v23

'Fear of the LORD leads to life, bringing security and protection from harm.'

MON 8 DEC

SOMEONE ONCE TOLD me that in some cultures it is common practice to put a child's hand in a fire briefly, to burn them slightly. The theory is that they will then be aware of what a fire can do and will be cautious with how they handle fire in future. In a way we could call this 'positive fear'; a survival instinct. Fear like this can help to prevent us from coming to harm. We are careful when we cross the road, because we fear the risk of being run over. We are cautious around wild animals because we know they can be dangerous.

A few weeks ago we thought a lot about fear and the Bible's command not to be afraid. However, the Bible also tells us that we should fear God, as we read yesterday. Today's proverb reminds us of the importance of fearing God in bringing us security and protection. Fear of worldly things (eg rejection from people, losing something expensive) holds us back from the life God wants for us. Fear of God is wise and life-giving. This is the one fear that can bring us life, security and peace.

THINK

How do you respond to the idea of fearing God? Do you embrace it or hold back? How does this decision affect your life?

TUES 9 DEC

READ:
GENESIS 3:1–10

KEY VERSE
v10

'He replied, "I heard you walking in the garden, so I hid. I was afraid because I was naked."'

I HAVE A friend who was expelled from school. To this day, her parents still don't know! She managed to hide the letters that her school sent home and convinced her parents to send her to a different school because she was being bullied. She was thoroughly ashamed of herself and this made her tie herself in knots to hide the truth.

This is very similar to Adam and Eve's situation. Adam says he's afraid, not because of his action in disobeying God, in itself, but because he's naked (v10), even though he was naked long before he did anything wrong. He's not just feeling guilty about what he's done; he's feeling ashamed of who he is. This shame makes Adam afraid of God.

When we know we've done something wrong, we often feel ashamed. This shame can make us afraid of God – we don't want Him to see us for who we are. But of course, trying to hide from God is pointless. He already knows where we are and what we've done. He knows who we are too, but He doesn't define us based on the things we've got wrong. Instead of hiding from God, let's realise that God sees us and knows us and let's accept the forgiveness that He offers us.

PRAY

Is there anything that makes you feel ashamed? Don't keep God at a distance. Talk to God about what you've done and how you feel. Say sorry and receive His forgiveness.

READ:
HEBREWS 12:14–29

KEY VERSE v28

'let us be thankful and please God by worshiping him with holy fear and awe.'

WED 10 DEC

IF YOU'VE BEEN a Christian for a while, it's easy to get used to having God around. The problem with that is that you can find yourself taking God for granted. We can often lose sight of how awesome God is and just treat Him like part of the furniture of our lives. I know that's certainly been true for me at times.

The great danger of taking God for granted is that we stop listening to Him. This is what the writer of Hebrews warns us against. And the answer to this danger is a healthy dose of holy fear! The writer presents us with a picture of Moses on Mount Sinai, where he received the Ten Commandments. It's a terrifying place of 'flaming fire, darkness, gloom, and whirlwind' (v18), a place where God's power and holiness are utterly awesome.

But this awe-inspiring God means to use His power to bless us, not to terrify us. He wants to give us 'a Kingdom that is unshakeable' (v28). Holy fear means recognising how incredibly powerful God is, but also that He loves us and wants to bless us. These truths should prompt us to take God seriously! We should never forget to listen to God's commands and act on them.

→ CHALLENGE

Have you got used to having God around? Reflect on how awesome He is. Remember what He's done for you in the past and what He can do with your future. Commit to listen to Him and worship Him with 'holy fear'.

READ:
MATTHEW 8:28-34

THURS 11 DEC

KEY VERSE
v34

'Then the entire town came out to meet Jesus, but they begged him to go away and leave them alone.'

TODAY'S READING HAS often baffled me. The town in this passage was terrorised by two men who were possessed by demons. We are told that these two men were 'so violent' that no one could go through the area of the cemetery where they lived (v28). But yet, when Jesus drives out the demons, 'the entire town came out to meet Jesus, but they begged him to go away and leave them alone' (v34).

So what on earth made them so anxious to get rid of Jesus? Well, it's simple really. They owned the pigs. When the newly demon-possessed pigs plummeted over the cliff and drowned in the lake, the people's livelihood went with them. The people couldn't stand it that Jesus was making a mess of their financial interests and they begged Him to leave them out of fear that He might disturb other areas of their lives too. They saw an incredible example of God's purpose to bring freedom and wholeness, but they opposed it out of self-interest. They were so used to their comfortable lifestyle that they were afraid of losing it, even for something as wonderful as the Kingdom of God.

CHALLENGE
Is there anything great that God wants to do in your life, which you're saying 'no' to because you're afraid of what it might cost you? Pray and ask God to help you let go of your fear.

READ:
DEUTERONOMY 13:1-5

FRI 12 DEC

KEY VERSE v4

'Serve only the LORD your God and fear him alone. Obey his commands, listen to his voice, and cling to him.'

IMAGINE YOU ARE in church one Sunday when someone rushes in with a gun. They tell the congregation that they are going to shoot anyone who says they are a Christian. What do you do? Do you admit to being a Christian and risk losing your life? Or do you save yourself by denying it all?

Thankfully, we rarely hear of people's lives being threatened in the UK because of their Christian beliefs. However, this does not mean that we don't have fears associated with what people think of our beliefs. Perhaps you are afraid that people will exclude you or tease you for your Christian faith. Perhaps you're afraid that they'll try and argue against your beliefs and you won't know the right words to say in response.

Today's key verse reminds us to fear God over and above others. God is the only one whose opinion should really matter to us. He wants the very best for us and knows the right path for us to follow.

PRAY

Spend some time praying for Christians around the world who are persecuted. Ask God to help them stay strong when facing hardship. Pray for yourself too, that God will help you stay faithful to Him in all circumstances.

WEEKEND
13/14 DEC

READ: MATTHEW 25:14–30

KEY VERSE
v15
'He gave five bags of silver to one, two bags of silver to another, and one bag of silver to the last'

WHAT WOULD YOU do if you knew you could not fail? Although there might be many things you would choose to do, I wonder if one thing would be sharing the gospel with your friends. If you knew for sure that they would not ridicule you or ignore you, would you be more likely to share your faith with them?

If you're anything like me, then when you're in a situation where a tricky question has been asked or someone is looking for someone to help complete a difficult task, you look down and try to avoid eye contact. I often feel like I would rather blend into the background than be singled out for a duty I may not be able to manage or a question I may not be able to answer. Perhaps this was how the third servant in today's reading felt.

Rather than investing the money, he hid it out of fear that he would lose it and get in trouble with his master. In essence, he was worried about failing. I confess that I have some sympathy for him. But let's think for a moment about what Jesus is trying to tell us through this story.

Rather than silver, God has blessed us with different gifts. Perhaps it is the gift of hospitality, teaching or compassion. He wants us to use the gifts to serve Him and to reach out to others around us. One day we will have to answer to Him for what we did with these gifts He gave us. It's easy to let fear put us off using our gifts, or to use fear as an excuse for laziness. But respect for God – holy fear – should motivate us to serve Him as best we can in everything.

THINK

What gifts has God given you? Are you using these gifts as much as you could be, doing as God would want you to do? What do you fear most – failing in your attempts to use these gifts or letting God down by not attempting to use them?

MON 15 DEC

READ:
MATTHEW 14:22–36

KEY VERSE
v29

'"Yes, come," Jesus said. So Peter went over the side of the boat and walked on the water toward Jesus.'

HAVE YOU EVER felt that God was calling you to get out of your comfort zone and do something incredible? Some friends of mine are about to do just that as they are preparing to move out to Afghanistan with their two-year-old daughter to begin a new life there, working with local communities.

In today's reading, Peter is being told to get out of a boat in the middle of a stormy lake. Of course this is an amazing miracle. But what I think is really remarkable is the fact that it was Peter's suggestion in the first place! He had the courage and the faith to ask Jesus to help him do something that seemed impossible and Jesus responded by giving him the supernatural ability to do it. It's only when Peter's faith started to waver that his ability to walk on water did too.

Throughout the Bible, and in particular the New Testament, we see examples of people who were empowered to do amazing things to honour God. And, we are told, this ability can be ours as well (John 14:12).

CHALLENGE
Do you tend to stay in your comfort zone? Or are you looking out for opportunities to serve God, even if it might seem crazy? How do you respond when you feel God calling you to do something? Do you trust Him and go for it or do you avoid it out of fear?

READ:
MATTHEW 26:36-46

KEY VERSE
v39

'If it is possible, let this cup of suffering be taken away from me. Yet I want your will to be done, not mine.'

TUES 16 DEC

MY SISTER-IN-LAW IS an amazing lady. She works as a children's nurse in a cancer hospital. The other day she was telling me about a young boy who had told her he was scared of dying. Sadly, for this boy, death was a reality and was something that he faced only a few days later.

In today's reading, Jesus is facing death. And it is not just any death, but the horrific ordeal of crucifixion. If there was ever a time to feel afraid, I imagine Jesus experienced it now. The way in which He deals with His fear is truly an inspiration. Even at this terrifying time, He prays to God, 'Yet I want your will to be done, not mine.' How often are we able to pray like this? When I find myself in a situation that I find scary, I generally look for a way out!

Like Jesus, we can be honest with God. We can ask Him to take away our struggles. But if it is His will for us to endure them, we can know that He will use them for good. Jesus saved us all through His death and resurrection – this certainly brought glory to God!

PRAY

Father, thank You for the example that Jesus set for us. Thank You that He was willing to do Your will, even when that was a terrifying prospect. Help me to be more like Jesus, seeking to do Your will, whatever situation I find myself in. Amen.

WED 17 DEC

READ:
ACTS 9:1–19

KEY VERSE
v13
'But Lord ... I've heard many people talk about the terrible things this man has done to the believers in Jerusalem!'

I CAN SYMPATHISE with Ananias' initial reaction. Saul was a notorious persecutor of Christians. As one of Jesus' followers, Ananias was understandably reluctant to go and seek out a man like Saul. But, thankfully, he put his fear to one side and obeyed what God was telling him to do.

Many of us have been hurt by people in the past. Perhaps we have fallen out with one of our closest friends or have been exploited by somebody we thought cared about us. These hurts can make us afraid. Sometimes we might fear coming face to face with that person again. Or we might fear getting too close to somebody else in case they hurt us in that way as well. These fears are not God's plan for us.

When we hold on to past hurts and resentments, we harden our hearts and limit what God can do in that area of our lives. Perhaps we know that God is asking us to forgive or seek reconciliation but we try to push that away, because it might hurt to open up old wounds. But God does not call us to do these things alone: He promises us that He is with us, no matter what.

CHALLENGE
Is there somebody who you are struggling to forgive? Ask God to help you overcome your fear of dealing with this and commit to doing something about it.

READ:
EPHESIANS 4:21–32

KEY VERSE v31

'Get rid of all bitterness, rage, anger, harsh words, and slander, as well as all types of evil behavior.'

THURS 18 DEC

A FEW WEEKS ago, I was in a children's soft play centre when a family arrived with a teenager with special needs. This teenage boy started playing with the toddlers and was obviously having a great time. Some parents were fine with this, whereas others were clearly concerned. Not only was the boy significantly larger than the other children, but his language was also rather rude. It was apparent that some parents feared what impact this boy's influence would have on their own children.

Our fear can lead us to treat other people in ways we might later regret. Rather than overreacting because of our fear or prejudice, we should take a while to stop and think about how Jesus feels about this particular person or group of people. Fear rarely has a positive effect on the person we fear, or on ourselves. It causes conflict and friction amongst people – exactly the sort of things God would have us avoid. So this sort of fear is destructive. But when we keep our focus on Jesus and let Him lead us, our fears cannot control us.

THINK

Think about who you fear. It might be a particular person or perhaps a certain type of person. Why do you have this fear? What could you do about it? Pray about it now.

READ:
JOSHUA 1:1–9

KEY VERSE
v9

'This is my command—be strong and courageous! Do not be afraid ... For the LORD your God is with you wherever you go.'

APPARENTLY, THERE ARE now 3.2 million CCTV cameras in the UK. CCTV cameras can serve two valuable purposes. On the one hand, they help protect normal citizens, looking out for their safety. On the other hand, these cameras act as a deterrent; they can put would-be criminals off doing the wrong thing, in case they get caught. Some people see CCTV as something to fear. Others are grateful for it.

God's Word and instructions, as contained in the Bible, should provide us with an essential tool against fear. However, too many people get the wrong idea about it. They see God's rules in the Bible as a way of scaring us into submission. But this is certainly not the case! God has given us His rules and guidance, not because He is a heavenly tyrant, but because He wants the best for us.

When we live the way that God intended us to live, we have no need to fear. He is on our side and knows what is best for us. Today's passage reminds us that God is always there with us, not spying on us in the hope that we trip up, but to stand alongside us in the trials that we face, giving us strength and courage.

PRAY

Lord God, thank You for being with me, wherever I go and whatever I'm doing. Please help me to always listen to Your voice, not my own fear. Amen.

PT3

READ: GENESIS 1:26–28

KEY VERSE V26

'Then God said, "Let us make human beings in our image, to be like us."'

GOD

THE NATURE AND CHARACTER OF GOD

KNOWING GOD

WEEKEND 20/21 DEC

IN OUR SERIES on the 'Nature and Character of God', we've already covered a lot of ground looking at God's love and power. Now we turn our attention to how we can develop our relationship with God. It's nothing short of mind-blowing to realise that our God, who is infinitely powerful and infinitely loving, wants to know each of us

CONTINUED▶

CONTINUED

personally. Over the next week and a half, we'll think about how we can know God better.

A good place to start is to understand that God created us to be like Him. He made each of us with the potential to speak, act and feel in the same ways as He does. So when we look at ourselves and at other people we catch a little glimpse of what God is like. Of course, we're not exactly like God right now, because our flaws, our mistakes and our selfishness get in the way.

Imagine yourself as a mirror. When God looks in the mirror, He sees His reflection. But years of misuse and neglect have made the mirror broken and dirty. God has to repair and clean it, until eventually He can see a clear reflection of Himself. In heaven, we will be made perfect and we will clearly reflect God's glory. This is our destiny. But, in the meantime, the better we get to know God, the more time we spend with Him, reading the Bible, praying and listening to Him, the more we become like Him. Little by little, in our words, our actions and our thoughts, we start to look more like the God who created us.

THINK
Take an honest look at your words, your actions and your thoughts. Is there any part of your life that you know needs to change? Ask God to help you become more like Him in this area.

READ:
LEVITICUS 19:1–10

KEY VERSE
v2

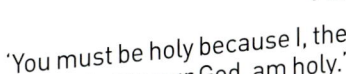

'You must be holy because I, the LORD your God, am holy.'

MON 22 DEC

BECAUSE GOD IS holy and perfect, we must be holy and perfect in order to know Him and be in His presence. In the Old Testament Law (of which Leviticus is a part), God gives an incredibly detailed list of commands which the Israelites had to follow in order to please Him. The Law includes regulations for sacrifices that people would have to offer whenever they slipped up and disobeyed one of the commands. God knows that human beings are imperfect and will sin and make mistakes, so His Law includes instructions on what to do when people break it!

So we're left with an awkward situation. We must be holy in order to know God, but in our imperfect state holiness is impossible. Fortunately, God has an answer. God chooses to make us holy. (Tomorrow we'll look at how that works.) But once God has dealt with our sin and made us holy this change should be noticeable in our actions. So we need to ask ourselves: do my actions show that I am holy? This doesn't mean that we need to wear sackcloth and eat locusts, but when people look at our lifestyle they should see that we're different.

THINK

Does your lifestyle show that you're holy? Is there anything that you know you need to change?

TUES 23 DEC

READ:
ROMANS 5:12–21

KEY VERSE
v19

'Because one person disobeyed God, many became sinners. But because one other person obeyed God, many will be made righteous.'

AS I WRITE this, I've just seen in the news that a man in Switzerland has racked up a record-breaking fine of £180,000 for speeding. The guy was reportedly caught driving his Ferrari through a village at 137km/h. I suppose the court decided that if he was rich enough to afford a Ferrari, he was rich enough to pay a good hefty fine. But imagine if this were you. Imagine you'd been caught driving too fast and had been given a fine of £180,000. Is there any way you could pay that? Probably not.

In the same way, each of us really does face a huge punishment. Because of our sins – the things we do that go against what God wants for us – we each deserve to be punished. In fact the Bible tells us that the punishment we deserve is death (see Rom. 6:23). But Jesus does something amazing. He chooses to take this punishment Himself. The punishment hanging over us is so huge there's no way we can pay it. (We mentioned yesterday that it's impossible for us to make ourselves holy.) But Jesus, the Son of God, takes our punishment, wipes away our sin and makes us right with God.

PRAY

Lord Jesus, thank You for dying so that I could be free from sin and right with God. Please help me to be holy; to live in a way which shows I'm thankful for what You've done for me. Amen.

READ:
MARK 1:29–39

KEY VERSE
v35

'Before daybreak the next morning, Jesus got up and went out to an isolated place to pray.'

WED 24 DEC

I ONCE WENT camping for a weekend with some friends. We packed up tents, sleeping bags and a bit of food and headed off into the forest. We wanted to get into the wilderness – away from the city and the pressures of life for a while. It was a lot of fun and a very liberating experience, but the best part of the weekend was Sunday morning. We each left the campsite individually and wandered off into the forest on our own. We allowed a couple of hours to think and pray alone. When we came back together, every single one of us had heard God speaking to us.

It's difficult to pray meaningfully and hear God speaking in the hustle and bustle of everyday life. To get closer to God, it really helps if we do what Jesus Himself did – spend quality time alone with His Father in heaven. This might mean praying in your room early in the morning or before you go to bed. It might mean going for a walk at lunchtime. It certainly means finding somewhere you won't be disturbed, and taking your time praying and listening.

→ CHALLENGE

How can you make quality time with God? Where and when can you arrange to be alone with Him?

THURS 25 DEC

READ:
GENESIS 2:1–3

KEY VERSE
v3

'God blessed the seventh day and declared it holy, because it was the day when he rested from all his work of creation.'

WHEN I WAS at college, one of my friends never did any work on Sundays. At the time I thought it was just a bit strange. I knew about the idea of a Sabbath but thought it was a bit old-fashioned. That didn't still matter at the beginning of the twenty-first century, surely?

Later, I found out the hard way why taking a Sabbath is really important. I'd been working hard for weeks and this culminated in a training event on a Saturday. The event lasted all day, and I was then busy in the evening too. I woke up on Sunday morning feeling absolutely dreadful. I realised I was on the verge of making myself ill by overworking. I spent that day resting, not because I chose to, but because I had to! If I'd been wiser about taking time out to rest during the previous weeks I'd have been in a much healthier state.

God didn't just rest on the seventh day because He thought it was a nice idea. He set an example to us because He knows that we need to take a day a week to rest, for the good of our physical, mental and spiritual health. We all need a day a week that is set aside for resting, spending time with God and having fun. If we want to know God better, taking a Sabbath every week is a good way to start.

CHALLENGE
Today, enjoy a rest, eat some good food and spend some quality time with God. Happy Christmas!

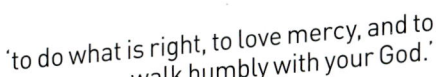

FRI 26 DEC

'to do what is right, to love mercy, and to walk humbly with your God.'

BUYING A SOFA seemed such a good idea – a nice comfortable place to sit while watching TV. Lovely. So off I went to my local furniture superstore. Wandering amongst all the sofas and armchairs was fun, seeing which one took my fancy. I made my choice, but the helpful sales assistant explained that there was some paperwork to deal with. To get my sofa I'd need to sign a credit agreement, including pages and pages of small print. I couldn't face reading it all, so I just signed and hoped for the best (not something I'd advise you to do!). Had I read the whole agreement, I'd never have remembered every single clause. But in the end it was simple – if I made my monthly payments on time, the sofa was mine.

The Old Testament Law contains 613 individual commands. In Jesus' time, people tied themselves in knots to obey every last one of them. It's remarkable that they managed to remember all 613 commands, let alone tried to follow them all. It makes knowing God seem so complicated. But Micah makes it beautifully simple: 'do what is right … love mercy … walk humbly with your God'. In other words, the whole Law is summed up as: 'Love God, love people and do what you know is right.'

PRAY

Lord, thank You that knowing You is not complicated. Please help me to love You, love people and do what I know is right. Amen.

WEEKEND
27/28 DEC

READ:
AMOS 5:21–24

KEY VERSE
v24

'Instead, I want to see a mighty flood of justice, an endless river of righteous living.'

ACCORDING TO UNICEF: 'The world has enough food for every child, yet not every child has enough food to live.'* 22,000 children die each day due to poverty. Almost half the population of the world – over three billion people – live on less than US$2.50 a day. 1.1 billion people in developing countries have inadequate access to water; and 2.6 billion lack basic sanitation. This is unjust, this is preventable; something has to be done.

While Amos is writing, poverty and injustice are rife in Israel. And yet, the people of Israel are doing nothing about these huge problems. They are still worshipping God with their words, but their actions aren't backing up their words. They're showing no concern at all for the people around them who are suffering. God can't stand it. He won't accept Israel's sacrifices or take any notice of their worship songs, because these things are empty and meaningless unless the people take action for justice.

Times change, but we're in danger of behaving just like the Israelites did, thousands of years ago. The poor, marginalised and forgotten are all around us, wherever we go in the world. Church services are great but, when we're surrounded by billions of suffering people, singing sweetly in church is meaningless if we do nothing to help them. God wants justice far more than empty words. Our worship must include acting to help the poor and oppressed.

CHALLENGE

Do something to make a 'mighty flood of justice' happen. Raise money for a charity. Help out with a soup kitchen for homeless people. Join a mission team to a developing country. Just do whatever you can. You might not change the world for billions of people, but in God's name you can change the world for someone.

---

*www.unicef.org.uk

MON 29 DEC

READ:
JOHN 14:15–27

KEY VERSE
v16
'I will ask the Father, and he will give you another Advocate, who will never leave you.'

AFTER I LEFT college I spent two years as a volunteer youth worker. For a year of this I was on a placement with a church in London. I loved the church and was sorry to have to leave at the end of the year. I decided to leave something behind to remind everyone of me. So I photocopied my face and pinned the result to the church's notice board! It might sound stupid, but it worked. There was no way the church could forget me with my face enlarged to A3 size staring at them from the notice board.

When Jesus was about to leave His disciples, before being crucified, He had a slightly more helpful idea of something He could leave behind. Or, more accurately, Someone He could leave behind. God later fulfilled Jesus' promise and sent the Holy Spirit (see Acts 2). The Holy Spirit is God's presence with us. He is an advocate for us – a helper, comforter and adviser. In the same way that the Holy Spirit helped, comforted and guided a frightened and confused bunch of disciples, He is here to help us. And in the same way that He would never leave the disciples, He will never leave us.

THINK
Can you identify with the disciples? Is anything making you feel frightened or confused? Remember: the Holy Spirit is with you. He's here to help you and He will never leave you.

READ:
JOHN 16:12-15

KEY VERSE
v13

'When the Spirit of truth comes, he will guide you into all truth.'

TUES 30 DEC

ONE OF MY favourite films follows a cop who is trying to untangle the complicated sequence of events which led to a shooting and an explosion on a boat in a harbour. He brings a witness in for questioning, who explains that the whole episode was orchestrated by a crime lord called Keyser Soze. Between flashbacks from the previous few days, we hear the witness tell his story. But, as the film progresses, the plot becomes more and more complicated, we begin to realise that the witness might be misleading us, and we're left with many possibilities as to Keyser Soze's real identity. Along with the cop, we're left searching for the truth amongst a web of lies, half-truths and distractions.

In real life, we can sometimes find ourselves in a similar position. Lots of people claim to be telling the truth, but who can we trust? How can we know who God is? How can we be sure of what God is saying to us? In a world which claims that there are many versions of the truth, the Holy Spirit guides us to the definitive truth. The Holy Spirit is here with us to show us truth, teach us who God is and speak God's words to us.

PRAY

Ask the Holy Spirit to speak to you and guide you into truth. Wait and listen to see what He has to say to you.

WED 31 DEC

READ:
LUKE 1:26–38

KEY VERSE
v37

'For nothing is impossible with God.'

PERHAPS TODAY YOU'RE thinking about some New Year's resolutions. A couple of years ago, I was determined to write a novel. I think I made it as far as March before I gave up. Partly I ran out of ideas, and partly other pressures took over. I still have a one-third-finished novel sitting in the darkest recesses of my hard drive – and I haven't mustered the willpower to go back and finish it.

If, like me, you have a history of failed New Year's resolutions, it's tempting to go into the New Year thinking that nothing significant can change. If this sounds like you, it's important to remember that nothing is impossible with God. He created new life through a teenage virgin and an old woman well past child-bearing age. His power is unlimited. There is nothing He can't do. It might not be God's plan for me to write a novel, but if God decides to do something, it happens.

So why can't this be the year that all your friends become Christians, your family gets closer or your church sees God at work in new and fresh ways? As we start a new year, let's go into it with faith – and remember that nothing is impossible with God.

THINK

Look back over the past year. Reflect on what God has done for you. Look forward to next year. What do you want God to do for you? What can you do to love and serve Him better? Why can't this be the year it happens?

NOTES

METTLE SEPTEMBER–DECEMBER 2014

ORDER FORM

4 EASY WAYS TO ORDER:

1. For credit/debit card payment, call 01252 784710 (Mon–Fri, 9.30am – 5pm)
2. Visit our Online Store at www.cwr.org.uk/store
3. Send this form together with a cheque made payable to CWR to: CWR, Waverley Abbey House, Waverley Lane, Farnham, Surrey GU9 8EP
4. Visit a Christian bookshop

YOUR DETAILS

Name:

CWR ID No. (if known):

Address:

Postcode:

Telephone No. (for queries):

Email:

SUBSCRIPTIONS (NON DIRECT DEBIT)	QTY	PRICE (INCLUDING P&P)			TOTAL
Mettle (1yr, 3 issues)*		UK £14.50	Europe £16.60	Elsewhere £18.75*	
(Subscription prices already include postage and packing)				**TOTAL** **B**	

Please circle which four-month issue you would like your subscription to commence from:

Jan–Apr   **May–Aug**   **Sep–Dec**

*Order direct from CWR or from your National Distributor. For a full list of our National Distributors and contact details, visit www.cwr.org.uk/distributors

eSubscription and eBooks available. Visit **www.cwr.org.uk/mettle** for details.